STAGESCRIPTS

Winsome Pinnock
One Under

One Under

Winsome Pinnock was born in London. Her plays
include *The Wind of Change* (Half Moon Theatre),
Leave Taking (Liverpool Playhouse Studio; National
Theatre; Belgrade Theatre, Coventry; Lyric Studio,
Hammersmith), *Picture Palace* (Women's Theatre
Group), *A Hero's Welcome* (Women's Playhouse Trust
at the Royal Court Theatre Upstairs), *A Rock in Water*
(Royal Court Theatre Upstairs), *Talking in Tongues*
(Royal Court Theatre Upstairs), *Mules* (Clean Break
Theatre tour of British prisons; Royal Court Theatre
Upstairs; Magic Theatre, San Francisco; Mark Taper
Forum, Los Angeles) and *Water* (Tricycle Theatre).

Her television credits include *Chalk Face, EastEnders,
South of the Border* and the screenplay *Bitter Harvest*
(all BBC). Radio plays include adaptations of *Indiana*
by George Sand and *Let Them Call It Jazz* by Jean Rhys,
and the original plays *Her Father's Daughter* and *Water*
(adapted from her stage play). She has been writer-in-
residence at the Royal Court Theatre, the National
Theatre Studio, Clean Break Theatre/Holloway Prison
and the Tricycle Theatre. Awards include the George
Devine Award, Thames TV Playwrights' Scheme Award
for Best Play of the Year 1991, the Unity Theatre Trust
Award, and runner-up for the Susan Smith Blackburn
Award. She has been Judith E. Wilson Senior Visiting
Fellow at Cambridge University and is currently part-
time lecturer in creative writing at London Metropolitan
University.

WINSOME PINNOCK

One Under

faber and faber

First published in 2005
by Faber and Faber Limited
3 Queen Square London WC1N 3AU

Typeset by Country Setting, Kingsdown, Kent CT14 8ES
Printed in England by Intype London Ltd

A CIP record for this book
is available from the British Library

ISBN 0-571-21851-8

2 4 6 8 10 9 7 5 3 1

One Under was first presented as part of the 2004/5
'New Writing for New Audiences' season at the Tricycle
Theatre, London, on 7 February 2005. The cast was as
follows:

Christine Adie Allen
Zoe Doreene Blackstock
Cyrus Brian Bovell
Sonny Daon Broni
Ernest Geoffrey Burton
Nella Lynn Farleigh
Aleysha Sarah Ozeke
Mags Louise Yates

Director Jennie Darnell
Designer Matthew Wright
Lighting Designer Matthew Eagland
Sound Designer Fergus O'Hare

*The text published here went to press during rehearsals,
and may differ from that of the play in performance.*

Characters

Cyrus
a train driver, forty-five

Mags
a train driver

Sonny
thirty

Zoe
Sonny's foster-sister, late thirties

Nella
Zoe and Sonny's adoptive mother, late sixties

Christine
forty

Aleysha
nineteen

Ernest
a train cleaner, sixties

ONE UNDER

Bereavement can overshadow life:
the dead can destroy the living.

Joanna Briscoe

Act One

SCENE ONE

An office at an underground station. Cyrus sits in a chair, his head in his hands, and Mags stands next to him.

Mags Talk about lucky. She landed between the tracks, right under the pit. She said she could hear the train coming and she's thinking this is it, no images from her life flashing in front of her or nothing, just that sound of the train getting closer. All of a sudden she says she feels something slicing through her head and like a thunderbolt striking her and it's all sounds she reckons and her head's exploding and her body's vibrating and then it's gone. Nothing. Silence. She said the worst bit was having to climb back out again onto the platform. Embarrassing, she said it was. Luckily, there was hardly anyone there. Funny thing is that she's deliriously happy these days. She's married, got two kids and she can't think why she wanted to do it in the first place. What's the chances of that happening?

Cyrus Mags.

Mags You all right, Cy?

Cyrus Where's Ian?

Mags He'll be up in a minute.

Cyrus You said that half an hour ago. I'm going.

Mags You're not allowed down there, it's standard procedure.

Cyrus I'm going anyway.

Mags You can't. The police are on their way up.

Cyrus Police?

Mags Like I said, it's standard procedure.

Cyrus Fuck.

Mags It happens to all of us.

Cyrus Thanks.

Mags You're lucky to have got off for so long. I've had three. Imagine that. I was freaked out the first time. By the third I was grateful for the time off. Believe me, you've had it easy. The law of averages means that it should have happened to you years ago.

Cyrus You sound glad, Mags, that it finally happened to me.

Mags Don't be daft. I wouldn't wish it on my own worst enemy. It's no joke, is it?

Cyrus What do they want, the police?

Mags They'll want to take a statement.

Cyrus A statement?

Mags Everything you can remember.

Cyrus I can't remember nothing.

Mags It'll all come back to you.

Cyrus What will I tell them?

Mags They'll want to make sure there wasn't any foul play.

Cyrus I sounded the alarm.

Mags Not from you. Someone might have pushed him. It happens.

Cyrus I can't remember.

Mags Just make it up. Half the time they can't be bothered. It's all in a day's work for them.

Cyrus He fell.

Mags Don't tell them that, Cy. I'll bet there'll have to be an inquiry or something if you tell them that.

Cyrus Like he collapsed.

Mags You can always tell when they're gonna do it, can't you? It's like the crowd parts and they're standing there on their own and it's just you and them – just for a split second.

Cyrus Waving at me.

Mags Bloody nuisance if you ask me. Well, they are. I mean, why can't they do it in the privacy of their own homes? Pills or something.

Cyrus Maybe he recognised me.

Mags Don't be daft. They're sick, ent they? Why else would they do it? Look, he's brought the whole of London to a standstill.

Cyrus Picked me out or something.

Mags People like that are always on the lookout for an opportunity to create havoc. Attention-seekers.

Cyrus He was young.

Mags The young have got no patience, these days. First sign of a difficulty and they're off.

Cyrus Shut up, Mags.

Mags Eh?

Cyrus I can't hear myself. (*Cyrus gets up, paces.*) Why won't they tell us what's going on?

Mags It's a well-oiled machine down there, Cy. The minute it happens the place is heaving with people doing jobs you never knew existed. Go down there in an hour it'll be like nothing happened.

Cyrus Maybe he's one a the lucky ones.

Mags That's right.

Cyrus I'll bet he's embarrassed.

Mags Quite right too.

Cyrus Will you stay, Mags? When they come up?

Mags Course I will.

Cyrus I won't remember everything, see.

Mags I'll tell them what you told me.

Cyrus About him waving an' that.

Mags I phoned your house to let 'em know what happened. They're expecting you back early.

Cyrus What we gonna do, Mags?

Mags You'll be all right, Cyrus. Honestly. They'll give you time off, you know that, don't you? After a while you'll forget all about it. (*She takes the teacup away.*) Anderson goes to me, 'Take as much time as you need, Mags.' But I couldn't keep away from the place. One time I followed the night cleaners. They walk miles of tunnel every night, cleaning them tracks. I walked from Seven Sisters to King's Cross. I was covered in filth come the morning, but I loved it. There's a different smell down there at night-time.

    There's a knock at the door. Mags moves towards it.

You ready for this?

    Cyrus doesn't answer.

Cyrus

He doesn't answer.

Cy.

A dry-cleaner's. Christine is holding a huge bouquet. Aleysha watches, amused. There is a jacket on the counter.

Christine They're gorgeous. Ent they gorgeous, Al? You shouldn't have. You've made my day, Mr . . .

Sonny People call me Sonny.

Christine I come in here expecting to be elbow-deep in Mrs O'Casey's dirty underwear and instead I get this. (*She smells the bouquet.*) Gorgeous. Now, where shall we put them?

Sonny They're for you. Take them home.

Aleysha Can't I even look at them, then?

Sonny Put them in your flat.

Christine Oh, but they'll brighten the place up a bit. I'll put them here, shall I?

Aleysha They'll shrivel up and die you leave them there.

Christine I'll make sure they get plenty of water, won't I? Don't worry, Sonny, I'll take them home with me later. That's so kind of you. It's not often you get lovely things like this happen round here.

Sonny You deserve them. You're a nice person.

Aleysha Ooh.

Christine I'm not sure you'd agree with that, would you Al? I'm a hard taskmaster, ask her.

Sonny You're nice, I've seen you, nice to everybody what comes in here.

Aleysha He means that you allow people like Mad Mary to sit in here all day stinking the place out.

Christine I couldn't leave her out in the pouring rain, could I?

Aleysha She'll get us into trouble if she's not careful. You never know when Mr Chakravarty is going to drop in.

Sonny You've always got time for people.

Aleysha Is this some kind of community service award or what, then? Like they have on the telly?

Sonny Why not? For services rendered to her community.

Christine Don't be silly.

Sonny A-care-in-the-community service award goes to Christine.

Christine I'm embarrassed. Al, tell him what a cow I can be.

Aleysha She can be a right cow when she sets her mind to it. Mostly, though, she's too lazy to set her mind to it. Yesterday I had a two-hour lunch break and she didn't say nothing.

Christine I welcome every opportunity to get you out of my hair.

Aleysha Soft as a sponge, she is, and just as wet.

Sonny You pay attention to what people say.

Christine The flowers are lovely, Sonny, and I'm very pleased to accept your award.

Aleysha Speech speech speech.

Christine Oh, get away with you. Now, Sonny, when do you want this back?

Sonny Whenever.

Christine (*writing out ticket*) Shall we say tomorrow, then?

Aleysha It's two pound extra for the express service.

Christine Not for customers what bring me flowers, it's not.

Sonny Would you go out with me?

Aleysha giggles and has to turn around.

Today.

Christine It's a bit short notice, isn't it?

Sonny I won't be around tomorrow. I'm going away. Take it or leave it.

Christine We're rushed off our feet in here.

Sonny What about it? I'll take you anywhere you want to go.

Christine I'm afraid you've got the wrong idea about me. I'm a bitch really, ain't I, Al?

Aleysha If you say so.

Sonny You don't know the effect you have on people, do you? A few weeks ago I come in here down in the dumps. You sent me out of here feeling good about myself and I want to pay you back for that.

Christine I'm glad you felt that way, but it's got nothing to do with me. I just try to get on with people, that's all.

Sonny Course I understand you're reluctant. I mean, you only know me from a few conversations and that was merely scratching the surface. You don't know me from Adam.

Christine I can't even remember the conversation.

Sonny And you seemed so interested.

Aleysha It's a sales technique.

Sonny You mean you don't remember me? Never seen my face before?

Christine Sorry.

Sonny That's a shame.

Aleysha I remember you. Navy-blue sheets. Cotton.

Christine Aleysha's got a photographic memory. (*to Aleysha*) What was he wearing the last time he come in?

Aleysha A grey suit.

Christine Do you always wear a suit?

Sonny Pretty much.

Christine All right. I'll go out with you. Why not? I ain't got nothing planned.

Sonny You'll come?

Christine I said I would, didn't I? What time you picking me up? You are going to pick me up?

Sonny Did she say yes?

Aleysha She always says yes.

Christine Watch it, you.

Sonny I promise you, I've got no ulterior motives. I'm leaving the country and I'd simply like to spend some time with you before I leave. My treat. I'll pick you up here at 12.30. That's when you take lunch, ennit?

Christine You're asking me out to lunch?

Sonny Is that all right?

Christine That'll be lovely. I won't be able to change out of my jeans or nothing, though.

Sonny You look fantastic just as you are. You always do.

Aleysha Not taking her to the Ritz, then?

Sonny She'd fit in wherever I took her.

Christine I don't mind where we go.

Sonny Just relax and let me surprise you.

Christine If you say so.

Sonny Let me take care of things, just for the afternoon.

SCENE THREE

A train carriage. Cyrus is asleep. Ernest, a cleaner, is trying to rouse him.

Ernest Come on, man, train reach. End of the line.

Cyrus mumbles something.

Come nuh, man. Some of us wants to get home to we sweet sweet bed and we not so sweet wife.

Cyrus mumbles again.

What you say? You say what?

He shakes Cyrus gently. This has no effect so he looks around to make sure no one can see him and shakes him more roughly. Cyrus wakes.

End of the line, man, end of the line.

Cyrus Eh?

Ernest Train reach.

Cyrus Mmmmm.

Cyrus stands up and puts his jacket on, reaches for his bag.

Ernest You was talking in your sleep.

Cyrus What did I say?

Ernest You was using another language, talking in tongues.

Cyrus Yeah?

Ernest Like French or something.

Cyrus I don't speak French.

Ernest Greek or Spanish, something like that. (*pointing to a wallet on the floor*) Is that yours? You don't want to be losing that. A man who lose him wallet lose life itself.

Cyrus picks up his wallet. Searches it frantically. There's nothing in it.

Somebody rob you? You want me to call the police?

Cyrus No. No police. (*Cyrus stands, picks up his bag, looks out at the sign on the platform, seems confused.*) That sign says we're still at King's Cross.

Ernest What you think it should say? Trenchtown?

Cyrus But it can't be. We . . . What time is it?

Ernest (*looks at his watch*) Two twenty-five.

Cyrus Very funny. Now tell me, what time is it, really?

Ernest I already tell you, man. Let me get on with me work, nuh? Me have a train to clean and man want to go home.

Cyrus Just tell me when this train's leaving.

Ernest Where train fe go at this time in the morning?

Cyrus Let me see the time.

Ernest Man, you crazy? (*showing Cyrus his watch*) Two twenty-five a.m., all right? What's the matter with you? You just come outa coma or something?

Cyrus This train was scheduled to get to Leeds at 11.15 and you're trying to tell me that it's two o'clock in the morning and we're still at King's Cross?

Ernest What you harassing me for, feller? You see me a ticket inspector? (*Laughs, realisation dawning.*) Ah, now I see it. Oh God. (*Laughs.*)

Cyrus Don't laugh at me, man.

Ernest Take it easy, feller, nobody here trying to fuck you up. You been asleep, right? That musta been some deep sleep because this train already go to Leeds, bang on schedule. You must be sleep all the way and back. You a sleeper.

Cyrus I only closed my eyes for five minutes.

Ernest You closed your eyes for five hours.

Cyrus Jesus.

Ernest You have important business in Leeds?

Cyrus No, nothing important. I was just . . . I wanted to get away.

Ernest You musta bin tired.

Cyrus I haven't slept for weeks.

Ernest Then you needed it. You look in a bad way, boy. Let me guess what you running away from – a woman. I'm right, ennit? No point trying to get away from a woman if they don't want you to leave. Look how she pull you back already.

Cyrus She wouldn't want me back.

Ernest Oh, is she kick you out, then?

Cyrus That's none a your business. It was my decision to leave.

Ernest If you say so.

Cyrus I didn't even care where I was going. I just bought a ticket for the next train out.

Ernest Well, you ain't get very far, have you?

Cyrus She reckons I'm too preoccupied. What she mean by that?

Ernest They don't like it if you think about anything but them.

Cyrus stands.

Show you the door if you even look at another woman.

Cyrus You know a place I can stay round here? A hostel or a B&B? Somewhere cheap?

Ernest There must be plenty places. Ask anybody when you come outa the station. (*He looks at Cyrus.*) Here man, take this

He reaches into his pocket, takes out twenty pounds and hands it to Cyrus. Cyrus doesn't take it.

Go on, take it. Pay me back when you on your feet again.

Cyrus takes the money.

Cyrus You know what it feels like to kill a man?

Ernest What? Of course not. I'm God-fearing. (*Small laugh.*) Kill a man.

Cyrus I got to get out of here.

Ernest You done something wrong, son?

Cyrus Yes.

Ernest Is that what you really running away from?

Cyrus When's the next train?

Ernest You want to tell me what you done?

Cyrus What's it to you?

Ernest Man, you touchy. What do I care what you done? That's your business.

Cyrus Too right it's my business.

Ernest In any case, whatever it is, look like you ain't going anywhere, whether you like it or not. Look like the train bring you right back here to face up to it.

SCENE FOUR

A park. Christine and Sonny have just eaten lunch and are sitting on the grass, enjoying the sunshine.

Christine There's the criminals and the con men. I suppose the con men are kind of criminals, but only in the sense that what they do to you is criminal, but technically they're above the law. The criminals are above the law too – technically – but only just and some of them are very definitely underneath it, if you know what I mean. Mostly they're beyond it. Like one time this guy asks me to meet him at Heathrow Airport because he's going to take me away for three weeks in Antigua. I'm on the train, got the passports, tickets and everything, and the guy sat opposite me is reading the *Evening Standard* and I'm reading it with him, as you do, and guess whose mug shot's on the front page? Only my fella's. He's only gone and got himself arrested that morning for armed robbery. He must have thought he could fit a job in before we flew off – talk about over-committing yourself. Then there was the guy who had the police raiding my house in the middle of the night. He'd told me he was a naturopath. I should have known there was something funny from the way he drove his Rover. Bloody getaway driver. You could say I had it coming with the criminals, couldn't you, because the signs are always there if you look, but the con men are in a different class, really. They're very self-effacing – I suppose they'd have to be, wouldn't they? They always turn out to be madmen, mothers' boys or married. I'm getting better at spotting the way they try to disguise themselves: the madmen never look you in the eye, mothers' boys avoid taking you back to their place and the married ones – well, the married ones always cover their mouths when they're speaking because they don't want you to see their lips moving. Well, that's all behind me now. My days as a gangster's moll are well and truly over. My life's very quiet these days – just me, my little flat and the launderette. I am sorry. I've just broken two of the cardinal rules.

Sonny What are they then?

Christine Rule number one is don't talk too much about yourself on a date, always ask about him and rule number two is never to mention ex-boyfriends – although you did ask.

Sonny I did. And who needs rules anyway? This is your date, you can do whatever you want. And I like listening to you. You're interesting.

Christine Me? Interesting?

Sonny Yeah. You got a nice voice. It's very . . . vibrant.

Christine That's nice. Vibrant.

Sonny You've had a hard life.

Christine Says who?

Sonny You just told me you'd been screwed over by all these villains.

Christine I didn't say that.

Sonny Whatever way you look at it, it hasn't been easy, but you haven't had the stuffing knocked out of you.

Christine What you see is what you get.

Sonny How long you been at that launderette?

Christine Oh no you don't. I know what you're doing. Getting me to talk about myself so that I don't ask you anything about you.

Sonny I don't like talking about myself.

Christine That's what the con men say.

Sonny (*teasing*) What are you implying?

Christine Do you have a job?

Sonny Let's say I'm a salesman.

Christine What do you sell?

Sonny It doesn't matter about the product. It's the selling that counts.

Christine So, sell me something.

Sonny That's too easy. You're a pushover.

Christine Thank you very much.

Sonny All I'd have to do is tell you some sob story.

Christine Thanks.

Sonny Tell you that I had to find the money to treat my daughter for leukaemia.

Christine You wouldn't say that, would you?

Sonny And you'd buy the whole lot off me.

Christine Buy what?

Sonny Whatever I was selling, wouldn't you?

Christine I'm not that easy.

Sonny I'll bet you are.

Christine All right then, try me.

Sonny What, just like that? I don't go in for cold calling.

Christine See, not so easy, am I?

Pause.

Sonny What would you do if you won the lottery?

Christine Buy a house.

Sonny Apart from that?

Christine The same as everybody else: holidays, cars.

Sonny Something different.

Christine thinks for a while.

Christine There's this hotel on Russell Square. I'd book in there for weeks and live on room service. What would you do?

Sonny I'd spend it all on you.

Christine You've only just met me.

Sonny It's your lucky day. I'm your genie in the lamp.

Christine How many wishes do I get?

Sonny As many as you like. You can have anything you want. I'm sweating like a pig. I'll get us a drink in a minute.

Christine They say it's the hottest summer on record.

Sonny You should do this more often. You very rarely take a lunch break. Your boss takes you for granted.

Christine I take meself for granted (*A short pause. She gets up.*) I'd better be getting back.

Sonny So soon?

Christine We've been out for over an hour.

Sonny Don't go back.

Christine What, ever?

Sonny Spend the afternoon with me.

Christine Oh, an afternoon.

Sonny I'll take you on a magical mystery tour.

Christine I can't leave Aleysha on her own.

Sonny What if I told you I was on the run?

Christine On the run from what?

Sonny What do you think I'm on the run from?

Christine The police?

Sonny Would that do it?

Christine Do what?

Sonny Sell you the idea of playing truant for the afternoon? It would have to be gangsters, wouldn't it? That would do it for you, wouldn't it? Make spending time with me a more attractive prospect.

Christine Why would it have to be gangsters?

Sonny Because you're a gangster's moll.

Christine I'm a reformed character.

Sonny I stand corrected. You're not a gangster's moll. You're a gangster. The launderette is merely a front.

Christine A front for what?

Sonny Money-laundering.

Christine That makes sense. Where does the money come from?

Sonny Telephone fraud. You thought up a scam where you offer psychic counselling.

Christine That's not a scam. They're real counsellors on them lines.

Sonny Not on yours they're not.

Christine So, I'm a clever gangster.

Sonny Absolutely.

Christine And you're on the run.

Sonny That's right.

Christine Why?

Sonny I took some drugs money, and now a man with a scar is coming after me with a big gun.

Christine What's his name?

Sonny Big Al. They call him Capone. Do you know him?

Christine Should I?

Sonny He's a big name.

Christine I don't socialise in those circles any more.

Sonny I'm that scared I'm going to have to leave the country for a while, lie low until they've forgotten all about me.

Christine Where you going?

Sonny Spain. Portugal. I'll make my mind up when I get to the airport.

Christine So, tonight's your last evening in London?

Sonny That's right.

Christine And you want me to spend it with you?

Sonny Yes.

Christine Feeling lonely, are you?

Sonny I'm always lonely.

Christine Haven't you got any friends?

Sonny With friends like mine who needs enemies? Don't you feel sorry for me?

Christine I'll stay out with you for one more hour.

Sonny I'm hardly gonna be able to fulfil your wishes in one hour, am I?

Christine They might be very simple wishes.

Sonny You're a hard woman.

Christine One hour and that's your lot.

Sonny We'd better get a move on, then, hadn't we?

SCENE FIVE

A house in Tottenham. Nella's living room. Zoe busies herself around the room, tidying up. Nella is looking through the French windows into the (offstage) garden.

Nella It looks like he's doing a good job.

Zoe I could have done that for you. All you had to do was ask.

Nella You're always so busy.

Zoe Not that busy that I can't help my own mother out.

Nella Always running here and there. Always laden down with books. You'll get back trouble one day you're not careful.

Zoe I already have.

Nella Look at his muscles. Go on, have a look.

Zoe goes to the window.

You don't get muscles like that by staring at a computer all day long.

Zoe He must be freezing.

Nella He says he doesn't feel it.

Zoe turns away from the window.

Zoe I don't believe you, inviting strange men into the house.

Nella I wouldn't let just anybody in. I've got good instincts about people.

Zoe Like the 'Jehovah's Witnesses' who stole your jewellery.

Nella I knew there was something funny about them.

Zoe But you still let them in.

Nella There's always something funny about Jehovah's Witnesses. And he's not strange. He's part of my routine now. I can rely on him.

Zoe You mean you can't rely on me?

Nella Every Tuesday and Thursday at eleven o'clock.

Zoe Why doesn't he have a job?

Nella He's so disappointed if I haven't got anything for him to do. I'm running out of jobs to give him.

Zoe I must say the house is looking very good.

Nella He sorted out that damp patch on the wall.

Zoe (*noticing the wall*) Oh yes. And he doesn't ask you for any money for all this work?

Nella Not a penny.

Zoe He's got to be after *something*.

Nella Why must he? You've never trusted anyone, you. He's a good listener.

Zoe Is he?

Nella He doesn't get bored. He lets me talk.

Zoe What do you talk about?

Nella Everything.

Zoe You're a soft touch for waifs and strays. He could be anybody.

Nella He's got that wounded look to him.

Zoe You think all men have that wounded look.

Nella I don't think Robert has it. Robert looks more like somebody who'd do the wounding.

Zoe Now now, Nell. I might be allowed to say nasty things about Robert, but you're not. Now, stop salivating over half-naked men and have some lunch. I've made a stew with that beef and I'm going to sit and watch until you clear your plate.

Nella I knew my bad parenting would come back to haunt me one day.

Zoe There's enough there for you to put in the fridge for the rest of the week.

Nella How do you do that? I didn't even see you go in the kitchen.

Zoe You have to juggle when you've got kids, don't you?

Nella You didn't learn it from me.

Zoe I learnt it in spite of you.

Cyrus comes in from the garden.

Cyrus Do you want to take a look?

Nella steps out into the garden. Zoe stares at a self-conscious Cyrus.

Zoe Aren't you cold?

Cyrus It's very hot work.

Zoe You've done a very good job.

Cyrus Thanks.

Zoe I appreciate you helping my mother out. How much do we owe you?

Cyrus Nothing.

Zoe I think you should take something.

Cyrus It's on me.

Zoe You've just spent all afternoon cutting the garden and you don't want any money for it?

Cyrus I don't need paying.

Zoe Why not? You should be paid for your work.

Cyrus I enjoyed cutting Nella's garden.

Zoe And you're sure about the money?

Cyrus Yes. I'm sure. I need to wash my hands?

Zoe I know who you are.

Cyrus Who am I?

Zoe I remember you from the inquest.

Cyrus Are you going to say anything?

Zoe Do you think I should?

Cyrus I think you should do what you want.

Zoe I don't know what you want, why you've come here, but whatever it is you're up to I think you should stop right now. She's been through hell the last few months and I think you should leave her alone.

Cyrus I think that's up to her.

Zoe She'd be upset if she knew.

Cyrus So, why tell her?

Pause.

(*holding up his dirty hands*) My hands.

Zoe Through there.

Cyrus goes into the kitchen. Nella returns.

Nella That looks much better. Where is he?

Cyrus comes back in, putting his shirt on.

Cyrus All right, is it?

Nella Much better.

Zoe It's about time that garden was cut. The weeds were getting out of hand.

Nella It looks wonderful.

Cyrus You'll have to wait till spring till you can really get at them.

Nella You'll have something to eat with us, won't you, Cyrus? Zoe made a stew.

Zoe I'm afraid there isn't enough.

Nella Of course there's enough. Enough to last a whole week.

Zoe Enough to last *you* a whole week.

Nella You just said yourself we should pay him. We can at least give him a meal for all his efforts.

Cyrus (*to Nella*) I can't stop. I'm meeting someone.

Zoe Haven't you got a job?

Cyrus I been laid off.

Zoe Why?

Nella He sustained a back injury, didn't you, Cyrus?

Cyrus That's right.

Nella He's a car mechanic.

Zoe Really? A car mechanic. Where do you live?

Cyrus I'm staying at a hostel in Holloway.

Nella It sounds like a ghastly place.

Cyrus It's not too bad.

Nella I wonder whether you can do something about that kitchen table. It wobbles.

Zoe We shouldn't take advantage of his time any more. Robert can fix that for you.

Nella Robert? Are you joking? He needs to consult an instruction manual before he takes a pee.

Zoe That's not fair. You've never asked him to help you.

Nella And are you surprised?

Zoe I'll go and get that food. (*She goes.*)

Nella I had that dream about Sonny again last night. It seems so real: touching him, smelling his hair, feeling his heart beat very fast.

Cyrus And then you woke up.

Nella And *my* heart was beating very fast. It's ridiculous. In my dream I can run as fast as a thirty-year-old.

Cyrus You get there in time to save him.

Nella Not only can I run as fast as Linford Christie, but I'm also as strong as an ox.

Cyrus You manage to throw him to the ground and hold him there till the train pulls out of the station.

Nella And he's crying and thanking me and saying that he didn't really mean to do it, that he didn't mean to hurt me.

Cyrus It's a good dream.

Nella It leaves me with that empty-arms feeling.

Cyrus The funny thing is, Nella, I've started to have that dream too.

Nella You? Why would you have it? You didn't even know him.

Cyrus I suppose it's because I've got to know you so well.

Nella It's my dream.

Cyrus I know. I'm sorry. I didn't mean . . . I'm sorry.

Nella He came to see me, you know, the night before he . . .

Cyrus Yes, you said.

Nella He planted those bulbs in the garden. We had a lovely chat. I think it was his way of saying goodbye. Aren't they beautiful?

Zoe comes back in with two plates of food.

Cyrus I'll see you on Thursday, then.

Zoe I thought you were staying for dinner.

Nella I'll see you on Thursday, Cyrus.

Cyrus goes.

Your problem is that you're afraid of men.

Zoe How can I be? I'm married.

Nella I rest my case.

Zoe You're impossible, Nella.

Nella I like him.

Zoe You've got to stop this. You can't just keep taking people in off the streets.

Nella There's something about him. He makes me feel safe. You're not going to try to scare him off, are you?

Zoe Not if you don't want me to.

Nella Good. Now, let's eat.

SCENE SIX

Evening. A 'Contemporary Deluxe' suite in the Hotel Russell, Russell Square. Christine and Sonny enter the room.

Christine Oh. My. God.

Sonny You like?

Christine I'll say.

Sonny Good.

Christine It's perfect.

Sonny I was going to take you to a restaurant.

Christine This is better.

Sonny Private.

Christine I feel underdressed now.

Sonny You look all right.

Christine Outdone by the decor.

Sonny (*takes out money*) There was a shop in the lobby. Why don't you buy yourself something?

Christine I wouldn't dream of asking you to buy me a dress. You've already spent enough money on me.

Sonny I want to. It's a present.

Christine I don't want your money.

Sonny Relax. I'm not trying to buy you.

Christine looks around the room, puts her handbag and cardigan on the sofa.

Christine Did you win the lottery?

Sonny I'm a gangster on the run.

Christine I'm being serious.

Sonny What makes you think I'm joking?

Christine You're not a gangster.

Sonny How do you know?

Christine I want you to be serious.

Sonny Why?

Christine Just tell me.

Sonny The truth?

Christine Yes.

Sonny It's whatever you decide.

Christine Are you from a wealthy family?

Sonny Is that what you want?

Christine Stop making fun of me. I want to know.

Sonny You've spent all afternoon with me.

Christine So?

Sonny You know me.

Christine You're loaded. No wonder you never want to talk about yourself. I wouldn't talk about it either. You'd never know if people were after you or your money.

Sonny I don't find it a problem.

Christine It just goes to show, you never know who anybody is. You're very modest.

Sonny Am I?

Christine And well spoken. Not la-di-dah or nothing.

Sonny I went to college.

Christine Everyone's been to college.

Sonny Does it make a difference, me having money?

Christine Why should it?

Sonny It does sometimes, doesn't it?

Christine Not to me, it don't.

Sonny Liar.

   Christine disappears into a room.

(*looking at a menu*) What do you want to eat?

30

Christine (*offstage*) Jesus, have a look in here. This bathroom's as big as my flat. (*Christine comes out of the bathroom, her hands full of miniature shampoos and soaps, which she puts into her handbag.*) They've got everything in there – cleansers, toners.

Sonny You look like a little girl at a funfair.

Christine So, you come from a wealthy family?

Sonny Let's just say I got lucky.

Christine You mean your numbers came up?

Sonny Something like that.

Christine I don't believe in luck. I believe in destiny.

Sonny What's the difference?

Christine I reckon it's all planned out – everything – even before we're born. We think we're in control but we can't stop things happening to us.

Sonny Who does all the planning then?

Christine I'd be a millionaire if I knew that.

Sonny And why does one person – for instance, me – get a really good destiny and the other person – for example, you – get a really crap one?

Christine I suppose that's just down to the luck of the draw.

Sonny I thought you didn't believe in luck.

Christine I don't. And my life isn't crap. (*She goes into another room. Offstage*) Maybe some of us got a load a stuff to work out from another life.

Sonny (*moves to the window, looks out*) Karma.

Christine (*offstage*) What?

Sonny Karma. (*Draws the curtains then moves back into the room.*)

    Christine comes out of the bedroom.

Christine There's a four-poster bed in there. It's as big as the *Titanic*.

Sonny As long as there's no icebergs around we'll be all right then.

Christine I hope you're not getting any ideas.

Sonny I'm not trying to buy you.

Christine No?

Sonny I don't want anything from you.

Christine So, what's all this in aid of?

Sonny You can't believe that anyone would want to be that nice to you, can you?

Christine Depends what you mean by 'nice'.

Sonny Bad things happen all the time – just like that, out of the blue. You can cope with the bad things, you're used to it.

Christine What bad things?

Sonny But what about if something good was to happen to you – just like that, out of the blue – for someone to do something nice for you just because he likes you.

Christine I can't make head or tail of you. You're weird.

Sonny You can't stand it, can you?

Christine What do you want from me?

Sonny The question, Christine, is what do you want from me?

Christine I'm not stopping unless you tell me what's going on.

Pause.

Sonny All right. You want me to tell you what's really going on?

Christine It'd be a start.

Sonny You won't be alarmed?

Christine Takes a lot to shock me.

Sonny Take a look out the window. Go on.

Christine goes to the window, pulls the curtains apart and looks out.

Careful. You don't want them seeing you.

Christine Who?

Sonny Is there a man out there?

Christine I can't see no one.

Sonny He's seen you and done a runner.

Christine There's someone walking past.

Sonny What's he look like?

Christine Bald. Balding. Tracksuit and trainers.

Sonny That's him.

Christine Who is he?

Sonny Mr Walker. My minder.

Christine Why have you got a minder?

Sonny My little joke. He can't stand it. He's from the Home Office. He's looking after me till tomorrow. That's when they'll be shipping me out.

Christine Why? What you done?

Sonny That would be telling.

Christine You're a nark.

Sonny I redeemed myself.

Christine They're giving you a new life. Is that where you got the money?

Sonny And a brand new face.

Christine Never.

Sonny It hurts when I laugh.

Christine You're a nut. Is this true?

Sonny Don't you want it to be?

Christine Is that why the gangsters are after you? Where are they sending you?

Sonny Timbuktu.

Christine You said you was going to tell me the truth.

Cyrus What, don't you believe me?

Christine There's no such place.

Sonny So, you're staying?

Christine Maybe.

Sonny God, you're tricky. What is it? Maybe you're trying to buy me. That's it, isn't it?

Christine Hardly. I haven't got any money.

Sonny In order to make a sale a salesman has to submit himself to the desire of the client – it's in the manual. The money is a mere symbol to be passed back and forth between the buyer and the seller in a communion of souls. (*He empties his wallet, gives it to Christine.*) Have it. Have all of it.

*She is taken aback for a moment, but takes it and
stuffs it all in her jeans pockets.*

Better?

Christine nods.

So, what shall we eat? You choose.

Sonny picks up the menu and gives it to Christine.

Do you mind if I take my jacket off?

Christine watches him.

I'm sweating like a pig.

*She says nothing. Sonny takes off his jacket and hangs
it on the back of the chair.*

We can watch a film later if you fancy.

*Christine puts the menu down and walks towards the
bathroom.*

Taking a shower?

*Christine stops and takes a few notes from her pocket,
which she gives to Sonny.*

Christine I'll have the salmon.

*Christine goes into the bathroom, closes the door
behind her. Sonny sits.*

SCENE SEVEN

*Sonny's flat. Zoe stands in the doorway holding a bucket
full of cleaning utensils and a roll of black bin-liners.
Cyrus is standing in the middle of the room with a
sleeping bag on the floor at his feet.*

Zoe What are you doing here?

35

Cyrus I just woke up.

Zoe I can see that. How did you get in?

Cyrus Nella give me a key. She said I might as well stay here while it's empty. She hates the idea of the hostel.

Zoe What have you got there?

Cyrus What?

Zoe I just saw you put something in your pocket.

Cyrus It's mine.

Zoe I saw you put something in your pocket when I came in, as though you didn't want me to see it.

Cyrus Nella said it was up to me if I threw stuff away or kept it.

Zoe What was it?

Cyrus Nothing. I haven't taken anything.

Zoe Show me.

Cyrus What?

Zoe Empty your pockets and show me.

Cyrus Are you accusing me of something?

Zoe Go on.

Cyrus All right. Miss.

Cyrus empties his pockets, a piece of paper falls out. Zoe picks it up.

Zoe A dry-cleaning ticket.

Cyrus It's mine.

Zoe gives the ticket back to Cyrus.

Zoe You can't stay here.

Cyrus That's up to Nella.

Zoe It's not up to Nella.

Cyrus She wants me to take this place over.

Zoe Are you on the council waiting list?

Cyrus No.

Zoe I'm giving the keys back to the council. Have you got somewhere to go?

Cyrus Nella said she wanted me to sort this place out.

Zoe Don't worry about Nella.

Cyrus I don't want to let her down.

Zoe She knows that I'm taking care of things.

Cyrus She asked you to come round here weeks ago, but you never did.

Zoe I'm here now, aren't I? It doesn't look as though you've got very much done, anyway.

Cyrus I was going to make a start today.

Zoe And now you don't have to. Robert's coming round later. We'll get this lot cleared away in no time.

Cyrus Your husband.

Zoe That's right.

Cyrus You want me to leave, then?

Zoe If you don't mind. I'd like to make a start.

Cyrus I can help you.

Zoe That's very kind of you, but Rob'll be here soon.

Cyrus I'm sorry, but I can't leave. You see, I promised Nella I'd sort this out for her.

Zoe Well, you're off the hook, aren't you, because I'm going to deal with everything now.

Cyrus And I don't break my promises to Nella.

Zoe If you won't leave I'll have to call the police.

Cyrus Have you tried getting them out round here? They don't turn up unless it's a dire emergency and even then . . .

Zoe My husband will be here in a minute.

Cyrus That sounds like some kind of threat. It's not, is it?

Zoe I asked you to leave and you refused.

Cyrus This is my flat.

Zoe It's my brother's flat.

Cyrus Nella give it to me.

Zoe It isn't hers to give. Oh, what the hell. I'll just have to work around you, won't I? (*Starts to clean up.*)

Cyrus Don't touch that.

Zoe What?

Cyrus I don't want you to move anything. Everything's got to be left exactly as it is.

Zoe What are you talking about?

Cyrus Exactly as he left it.

Zoe It's rubbish.

Cyrus I don't want it touched.

Zoe Don't be ridiculous. The council want this place cleared as quickly as possible. It's got to be cleaned. It stinks.

Cyrus Not till I've done what Nella wants me to do.

Zoe I think you should leave before Robert gets here. He's not as tolerant as I am.

Cyrus Nella give me the key.

Zoe If she'd known who you were she'd never have done that in a million years.

Cyrus I'm the custodian.

Zoe The what? What do you mean?

Cyrus I'm looking after the place.

Zoe It doesn't need looking after. There's a family on the waiting list who'll be over the moon when this becomes free.

Cyrus You can't get rid of his stuff just like that, like it never meant anything.

Zoe If I find anything I think we should keep I'll give it to Nella, won't I?

Cyrus You can't touch anything. It's got to stay exactly as it is. Coming in here like you own the place. This is between me and Nella. And Sonny.

Zoe You're encouraging Nella's delusions. She told me the other day that she thought he might not be dead.

Cyrus He might not be.

Zoe Of course he's dead.

Cyrus I mean in a manner of speaking.

Zoe I don't care what manner you mean it in, he's dead and gone. I scattered his ashes.

Cyrus For an intelligent person you don't understand much, do you?

Zoe I don't understand the bullshit you've been peddling to poor old Nella and I have no idea why you would want to peddle it in the first place.

Cyrus He never left a note.

Zoe Most people don't. What would they say? Sorry? Well, we know that's not true, don't we?

Cyrus Perhaps he did leave a note.

Zoe Have you found something? Did you find a note?

Cyrus Yes.

Zoe Show it to me. I want to see it.

Cyrus holds his hands up and sweeps them to indicate the flat.

Cyrus He's left his shadow behind. Sit in here long enough and the room starts talking to you. Do you know what I mean? Look at what he's left on that table. He lights himself a cigarette, takes a drag on it. He pours himself a beer, takes a chug. He rests the cigarette on the side of the ashtray and lets it burn down. He only drinks half the glass.

Zoe What are you trying to say?

Cyrus He lets the cigarette burn down, only drinks half the can of beer – why does he do that?

Zoe You tell me.

Cyrus He let the cigarette burn down. He never put it out. Like I said, every picture tells a story.

Zoe You mean he meant to finish it. Is that what you mean?

Cyrus I'm being shown something, but I don't know what it means yet. I found this under his glass last night. (*Shows her the dry-cleaning ticket.*) Why would you put a dry-cleaning ticket under a half-empty glass like that unless you left it there knowing that someone would have to clear the glass away and find the ticket?

Zoe You think he left it deliberately?

Cyrus Someone was bound to find it.

Zoe To tell us something. Is that what you mean?

Cyrus Maybe.

Zoe To tell us what?

Cyrus I don't know.

Zoe But how could he be sure that anyone would find it?

Cyrus He knew I'd come.

Zoe You? Why you?

The telephone rings. Neither of them answers. We hear the ansaphone message.

Voice of Sonny Hi, this is Sonny. I can't take your call just now, but leave your name and number after the beep and I'll call you back.

Beep.

Voice of Robert Zoe, it's Robert. You must have got there by now. If you can hear me, pick up. I'm running late, Zo. My client was delayed so everything's backed up. I know I promised, but I'll help out tomorrow. See you later, Zo.

Beep. Pause.

Cyrus So, big bad hubby won't be calling round to throw me out after all.

Zoe (*attempting to placate Cyrus*) I'm sure this has all been very traumatic for you. Maybe even more so than for me and Nella. And we knew him.

Cyrus Are you saying I didn't?

Zoe It must be terrible, a stranger having this much impact on your life. I can't imagine what it must have been like for you. Suddenly out of the blue . . . it doesn't bear thinking about.

Cyrus He knew me. All those years thinking about him, imagining what must have become of him, longing for him, hoping he'd come and find me.

Zoe Find you?

Cyrus When Nella told me Sonny was adopted it blew my mind. All along I'd had this strange feeling that he'd chosen me for some reason.

Zoe You're not implying that Sonny . . .

Cyrus Yes, he's mine. Sonny's my boy.

Zoe You're joking.

Cyrus They said you couldn't raise a kid at fifteen. They said it was against the law. She was only fourteen, see. All this time I wanted to trace him, but they won't let you. He had to come to me.

Zoe If that's true, then what he did was horrible.

Cyrus How can we judge him when we have no idea why he did what he did?

Zoe He did it because he's selfish. He always has been. His response to a crisis was always to run away.

Cyrus So, you think there was a crisis?

Zoe There always was something going on with Sonny.

Cyrus Yeah? Well, to me this looks like a room he meant to come back to.

Zoe Are you saying that he might not have intended to . . .

Cyrus I don't know what he intended. All I know is that he called me here to find out.

Zoe Why you? Perhaps he meant for me to find the ticket.

Cyrus Nella said you hadn't spoken to him for ages.

Zoe We were very close when we were children. He always looked out for me.

Cyrus Yeah?

Zoe None of the other kids dared touch me. He'd be there in a flash with his fists up.

Cyrus See, I told him to look for me. The day we give him up I held him for hours. A little thing in my hand. I was a kiddy meself, still searching for conkers and ink stains on my fingers. Then the knocking on the door and me shouting about give me a bit of privacy and I whispered to him. I said, 'I'm your dad. Me. And when you're old enough you come and you find me.' I just want to do right by my boy.

Zoe Two weeks. I'll give you two weeks. After that I'm giving the keys back to the council.

Cyrus That's enough. Just give me the chance to find him. Give me a chance to find my boy.

SCENE EIGHT

The hotel room. Night. Sonny comes out of the bedroom, fully dressed. He puts his shoes on. He sits in a chair and pours himself a drink. Christine follows him out, dressed in a towelling robe. She sits and he passes her the glass. She drinks and passes it back to him. There is a very long pause.

Christine I'm dead.

Pause.

I've died and gone to heaven.

Pause.

I'm never going back to work. I'm going to stay here and let you fuck me all day and all night for the rest of my life.

Pause.

Did I tell you my mum used to work here as a cleaner? (*Corrects herself.*) Sorry, chambermaid.

Pause.

When you come, you . . .

Sonny Do you always talk about it after?

Christine Did I tell you it was my birthday?

Sonny Today?

Christine Did you know?

Sonny You should have said.

Christine I thought maybe you knew.

Sonny How would I know? How old are you?

Christine Guess.

Sonny Twenty-seven.

  Christine laughs.

Christine Don't be stupid.

Sonny You have the body of a twenty-seven-year-old.

Christine I'm thirty-eight.

Sonny You look younger.

Christine How old are you?

Sonny I'm ageless. Timeless.

Christine Let me guess – thirty-five. No, thirty-seven.

Sonny You're spot on.

Christine Thirty-five or thirty-seven?

Sonny You choose.

Christine Did you plan all this?

Sonny Is it really your birthday?

Christine Bet you booked this suite days ago, weeks ago probably.

Sonny That's a coincidence, isn't it?

Christine I'm flattered.

Sonny (*sings*) Happy birthday to you,

Christine There's no such thing as coincidence.

Sonny The body of a thirty-year-old.

Christine This is the best birthday I've had in ages. Did you?

Sonny Did I what?

Christine Plan all this.

Sonny What do you think?

Christine Aleysha reckons you've been stalking me, says she's seen you hanging around.

Sonny You like it.

Christine For all you knew it might have all gone tits-up.

Sonny It did.

Christine I might have thrown your flowers back in your face.

Sonny No.

Christine I might have said no when you asked me out.

Sonny Not you.

Christine Are you saying I'm easy?

Sonny You find it hard to say no.

Christine I find it easy to say yes.

Sonny That's what I mean.

Christine I open myself up to life.

Sonny Good for you.

Christine Are you laughing at me?

Sonny Of course not.

Christine I'm not like other people. I don't shut myself down.

Sonny Lucky for me.

Christine You were crying in there.

Sonny Was I?

Christine I've never had that happen to me before.

Sonny What, never?

Christine It's usually me who does the crying.

Sonny That figures.

Pause.

Christine When was the last time you went with someone?

Sonny I can't remember.

Christine Go on.

Sonny Months.

Christine How many months?

Sonny Six. You?

Christine A year.

They pass the drink back and forth.

Why were you crying?

Sonny It happens sometimes.

Christine I was really touched.

Sonny What do you mean, touched?

Christine I don't meet men who cry a lot.

Sonny I don't cry a lot.

Christine It means something, doesn't it?

Sonny What? What does it mean?

Christine It's significant. It means it matters.

Sonny What matters?

Christine Something. I don't know.

Sonny Look, what happened in there. It was nothing.

Christine Nothing? What do you mean?

Sonny I only did it because you wanted to. I wouldn't take advantage of you.

Christine You seduced me. You got me drunk.

Sonny I think you'll find that the seducer is always the seduced.

Christine I don't hear you complaining.

Sonny Because I'm not.

Christine Well then.

Sonny As long as it made you happy.

Christine I am.

Sonny As long as you understand that it was because you wanted it. Nothing more.

Christine I'm a grown-up. What, do you think I'm going to ask you to marry me?

Sonny My intentions towards you . . .

Christine I know. You're going away tomorrow. I might never see you again.

Sonny That's why I wanna get things straight.

Christine lies back on the sofa.

Make a habit of this do you? Sleeping with men you don't know?

Christine No, I do not.

Sonny You don't know anything about me.

Christine You don't know anything about *me*.

Sonny I could be anybody.

Christine But you're not, are you?

Sonny Who am I?

Christine Whoever you say you are.

Sonny Cool. Everything's cool, then. We both know where we stand. You've enjoyed yourself tonight. Everything was the way you wanted it. The hotel, you like this hotel?

Christine I said, didn't I?

Sonny Because I want to make you happy.

Christine For one night?

Sonny Why not?

Christine That's fine by me.

   Sonny paces.

Sonny This wasn't supposed to happen.

Christine Are you always this neurotic?

Sonny I didn't think you'd want this.

Christine (*teasing him*) Come off it. You had it all worked out, didn't you? This is what you was after all along.

Sonny Look at me. (*He holds Christine's chin.*) Let me see you. (*He looks at her face.*) Always a smile on your face, nothing ever upsets you, but your eyes tell a different story.

Christine I'm an open book, me.

Sonny Oh yeah?

Christine You'll be asking me did I come next.

Sonny Did you?

Christine (*laughing*) I can't believe you. What's it matter anyway? You'll never see me again after tonight.

Sonny Tell me why you're so sad.

Christine You're the one who was crying.

   Sonny nods. After a while he stands up, puts his jacket on.

Are you going somewhere?

Sonny Get some fags.

Christine You haven't smoked all day.

Sonny I had you to keep me occupied, didn't I?

Christine Ring room service and ask them to bring you some up.

Sonny I want to stretch my legs.

Christine (*a challenge almost*) Shall I come with you?

Sonny No.

Christine Don't go.

Sonny I need some fresh air.

Christine You're not coming back.

Sonny You have a really poor view of men.

Christine You've gone all shifty.

Sonny I'll be back. I promise.

Christine I've heard it all before.

Sonny Do you want me to get you anything?

Christine What am I supposed to do about all this? I can't afford to pay for it.

Sonny It's all taken care of. Why don't you go back to sleep?

Christine I want to be the one who leaves.

Sonny Whatever you say.

Christine Please don't go.

Sonny Don't beg, Christine. It doesn't suit you.

Christine I don't care. It's my birthday.

Sonny I'll bring something back for you. If I'm bringing something back I'm not leaving, am I?

Christine Jelly babies.

Sonny Jelly babies.

Christine A bag of green jelly babies.

Sonny All right.

Christine You said you'd do anything I wanted.

Sonny Of course.

Christine You'll come back?

Sonny Of course I'll come back. It's a promise.

Christine You'll be cursed if you don't. Remember what you said. It was a promise, remember.

Sonny stands for a moment. He nods, smiles and then leaves.

SCENE NINE

The dry-cleaner's. Present. Christine stands behind counter and Cyrus in front of it. Aleysha watches them, holding a jacket on a wire hanger, wrapped in cellophane.

Christine I'm sorry about when you come in before. It's just when you come to pick up that jacket I didn't know what was going on.

Cyrus I understand completely.

Christine I thought he'd sent you here for a laugh, to stick the boot in, you know. I didn't mean to have a go at you.

Cyrus I understand.

Christine And then when you told me that he . . . it was a bit of a shock.

Aleysha She hasn't stopped crying since this morning.

Christine You must have had him very young. You could pass for his brother.

Cyrus Do you think we look alike, then?

Christine It's more the way you carry yourself. You've got the same sort of air about you. I can't believe he did what you said. To think, he must have been planning it all that day.

Aleysha You don't half pick 'em, Chris. This is the worst though.

Christine He was a lovely bloke.

Aleysha You only went out with him the once.

Christine It doesn't matter that it was only the once. Sometimes you can tell straightaway, can't you?

Aleysha Tell what?

Christine I'm saying that sometimes you just hit it off with someone.

Cyrus Can I have it? The jacket?

Aleysha checks with Christine, who nods that it's okay to give Cyrus the jacket. Aleysha gives Cyrus the jacket. He impatiently tears at the cellophane and desperately searches the pockets, turning them inside out. He doesn't find anything and can't hide his disappointment.

Don't you take stuff out of the pockets before you clean them?

Christine If we find anything we take it out and put it back in the pocket after we've cleaned it.

Aleysha You wouldn't believe what some people carry in their pockets.

Christine Though we're very discreet.

Aleysha Some of the love letters are hilarious. We know everything about what's going on in this area.

Cyrus And you always do that?

Christine Was he supposed to leave something in there for you?

Aleysha There weren't no lottery tickets in there or nothing.

Christine She always checks the pockets.

Aleysha Found twenty quid once.

Christine What did you expect to find?

Cyrus I don't know. A note. Something.

Christine I'm very sorry. That must be terrible, not knowing why. You'd expect a note, wouldn't you? You want to say goodbye, don't you? I can't believe it. One minute he's standing there, the next minute he's gone.

Aleysha You're talking like you knew him. You only went out with him the once.

Christine I did know him. I was probably the last person to see him before he . . .

Aleysha He saw you coming.

Cyrus I'm sorry I had to be the one to bring you the news.

Aleysha Why do you think he picked her?

Cyrus shrugs.

They always pick her. (*She goes.*)

Cyrus If it's any consolation – and I'm sure it won't be much – from what you've told me I'm sure that you brought him some comfort in them last hours.

Christine Do you think I was his final request, like the men on Death Row who place orders for steak and chips?

53

Cyrus Don't think too badly of him.

Christine I don't. He was a genuinely nice bloke.

Cyrus Did he . . . did he . . . tell you anything?

Christine What like?

Cyrus Did he say anything about me?

Christine I don't think so. I can't remember. It's a terrible thing to lose a child. We're supposed to go first, aren't we? Sit down.

Cyrus I hardly knew him.

Christine I'd never have guessed he was going to . . . He had a good sense of humour.

Cyrus Did he?

Christine He liked a joke. He was playful. He made me laugh.

Cyrus Yes? A joker, was he? Tell me one of his jokes.

Christine He never told jokes, he was more . . . playful. He liked to pretend.

Cyrus I see. Perhaps I don't need to hear this.

Christine It was fun.

Cyrus I'll bet it was.

Christine I mean real pretence. Like kids, you know?

Cyrus I know what you mean – doctors and nurses an' that.

Christine He told me he was on the run from gangsters.

Cyrus He said that?

Christine It was a game.

Cyrus He came right out and told you he was on the run?

Christine He said they'd changed his face and everything.

Cyrus Who did?

Christine The Home Office. Said they'd given him a new identity and that it was his last night in London. It was his reward for confessing.

Cyrus Confessing to what?

Christine He didn't say. He had a fantastic imagination.

Cyrus He told you all this?

Christine He was playing with me.

Cyrus I get it. All the time I thought he'd left me some message in the jacket, but it wasn't about the jacket, was it? It was about you.

Christine Me?

Cyrus He told you something, something for me. What did he tell you?

Christine Nothing. I can't think. My mind's gone blank.

Cyrus He picked you out, give you a message for me. It won't be obvious because that's how he likes to play the game. He wants to make me work for the answers.

Christine What game? He never said nothing about you.

Cyrus He wouldn't would he? That'd be far too easy. I want you to tell me everything, everything that happened that night, everything he told you. Do you understand?

Christine Yes, yes, I think so.

Cyrus Good. So, come on, tell me everything.

End of Act One.

55

Act Two

SCENE ONE

Sonny's flat. Evening.

Cyrus Please. Come in. Sorry about the mess.

Christine enters the room, reluctantly. It is absolutely filthy.

Have a seat.

Christine looks around. She can't see a seat. Cyrus clears newspapers from the chair.

Christine It's all right. I think I'll stand.

Cyrus Cup of tea?

Christine You seem very . . . busy.

Cyrus It's no trouble. I just put the kettle on.

Christine Maybe later, eh?

Cyrus All right. If you're sure.

Christine My mum's brother used to live on this estate. He had a heel-repair bar on the West Green Road. He moved to Middlesex as soon as he got the money for a house. I haven't been round here for ages. I hardly recognised the place.

Cyrus They've done it up.

Christine You get a nice view across London standing on that balcony, don't you?

Cyrus You wanna see it at night, when all the lights come on.

Christine So what, you staying here?

Cyrus Just while I get everything sorted, you know.

Christine Did you want me to help you clear up?

Cyrus No way. Everything's got to stay exactly as it is.

Christine You won't be able to see anything soon. It'll all have decayed into some soupy black mess.

Cyrus It stays as it is.

Pause.

It's been a boon meeting you, Christine, a real vindication. I knew that ticket would lead to something, but I'd never have guessed what. Nights I've sat in this flat thinking, trying to put it all together. And then you turn up and everything starts to make sense.

Christine Yeah?

Pause.

Makes sense how?

Cyrus First I want you to open these. They arrived this morning.

Christine Why don't you open them?

Cyrus You're good luck, you. (*Christine regards Cyrus. She opens the first letter, reads.*)

Christine He owes five pounds on an overdue library book.

Cyrus Which book?

Christine *War and Peace.*

Cyrus I seen that somewhere. I'll have to have a read of that. There might be something in it.

Christine Like what?

Cyrus I won't know till I've read it, will I? Go on.

Christine opens the second letter.

Christine (*reads*) He's been approved in principle for a loan of up to fifty thousand pounds. All he has to do is ring this number in order to take advantage of low interest rates and nothing to pay till August. This isn't getting us very far, is it?

Cyrus Don't matter.

Christine Because you've worked it all out?

Cyrus That's right.

Pause. Cyrus grins.

Christine So, are you gonna tell me or what?

Cyrus He didn't want to jump. Someone forced him to.

Christine Who did?

Cyrus That bloke. That bloke you was telling me about.

Christine Which bloke?

Cyrus The one who was following him.

Christine You don't mean Mr Walker?

Cyrus That's him.

Christine You've got it all wrong. See, there weren't any gangsters, were there? He was having me on.

Cyrus Someone put him under so much pressure he felt he never had any choice.

Christine I think he was having me on about the Home Office.

Cyrus Of course he was, but why he did he tell you about being followed an' that?

Christine To make me feel better.

Cyrus Make you feel better?

Christine He said I seemed sad. He wanted to make me feel better.

Cyrus Why you?

Christine He said I was special, beautiful.

Cyrus says nothing.

I know. I know what you're thinking. I think it too.

Cyrus So, there might not have been a Mr Walker, not as such, but there might have been someone.

The phone starts ringing.

That story he told you.

Christine About the gangsters.

Cyrus He was playing a game you reckon, yeah?

The ansaphone comes on.

Voice of Sonny Hi, this is Sonny I can't take your call just now, but leave your name and number after the beep and I'll call you back.

Beep.

Zoe (*off*) Hello, it's Zoe. I've been trying to get in touch with you. Are you there? If you're there will you pick up the phone? You're not there. I've been thinking very carefully about what you told me last night and I have something to tell *you*. Can we meet? Not at the flat. It doesn't seem appropriate. Meet me at the café on the corner at, say, one tomorrow? Call me back if there's any problem. Otherwise I'll see you at one.

The phone beeps.

Christine Who is that?

Cyrus His sister.

Christine I never knew he had a sister. It's none of my business, is it? Poking my nose everywhere.

Cyrus You got a right to be here. You're a part of this now.

Christine She wants to meet you. She wants to talk to you about him. She look like him?

Cyrus A bit.

Christine She must be beside herself with grief.

Cyrus It don't show. She's tough.

Christine I shouldn't have come here. I'm intruding.

Cyrus Course you belong here.

Christine It should only be the family, shouldn't it?

Cyrus You are family.

Christine Did you tell her about me?

Cyrus Everything. I told her everything.

Christine And now she's got something to tell you.

Cyrus It's like the trail of breadcrumbs them smart kids left behind in that fairy tale. Every piece of bread leading me back to him. First there was that ticket, then I found you and you led me to Mr Walker. It all makes complete sense.

Christine Not to me it doesn't.

Cyrus His message is so clear. I can't believe we didn't understand it before. He sent you to let me know that there was someone behind it.

Christine You come in my shop. He sent you to me.

Cyrus I pieced it all together from what you told me. He said he was being followed. Maybe that was true. Maybe he had something they wanted. They couldn't touch him while you was with him, see.

Christine Are you blaming me?

Cyrus They had to wait until he was on his own.

Christine What happened to him had nothing to do with me. He had it all planned before he even come in my shop.

Cyrus He come back here, changed out of his suit, poured himself a drink and had a cigarette. Then something stopped him finishing his drink. Maybe he realised he was running out of time, that they was catching up with him. So he goes to see Nella.

Christine Who's Nella?

Cyrus Buries something in her garden.

Christine What?

Cyrus Whatever it is they're after. Then they catch up with him and he has to start running again. They run him under.

Christine That's terrible.

Cyrus Yes, it's terrible. Of course it may have happened a different way but I reckon I'm close. I can feel it. I want to find out who was responsible.

Christine What if they come after us?

61

Cyrus The puzzle's starting to make sense.

Christine I reckon we should leave well alone. I don't want to get involved.

Cyrus You've got no choice.

Christine I've got my own life to get on with. I don't want to get into trouble.

Cyrus He was in trouble. And he come to you to help him. He give you a message to pass on to me. He doesn't want us to forget him. At night I feel it. In this room – whispers, somebody's heartbeat. You never cut that psychic cord, do you? It's strong between a father and his son. He wants me to find out what happened to him, who was responsible. And I'm not gonna stop till I do what he wants. And when I find them, when I find the people who messed with my boy, there's gonna be hell to pay.

SCENE TWO

Hotel room. Sonny stands in the doorway.

Sonny It's very warm out there. Balmy.

Sonny comes into the room and shuts the door behind him.

Close your eyes you'd think you was in the Caribbean.

Christine Have a nice walk, did you?

Sonny London's a different animal at night, isn't it? That's when all the girls and boys come out to play.

Christine Mr Walker still out there?

Sonny The heat's getting to him.

Christine Been chatting to him, yeah?

Sonny He was fast asleep in his car, dead to the world. I'm surprised he hasn't woken himself up with his snoring.

Christine It's been a long day for him. You've kept him on his toes.

Sonny I should think he's dehydrated. I've told him before he doesn't drink enough water, doesn't look after himself.

Christine You took your time.

Sonny Are you angry with me?

Christine Why should I be? I've only been sat up half the night waiting for you to come back.

Sonny Don't exaggerate.

Christine And you don't mess me about. Who do you think you are, keeping me waiting?

Sonny I didn't mean to upset you.

Christine You love the night-time. Well, I don't. I feel like things are crowding in on me at night.

Sonny What things?

Christine Thoughts. Life. Everything.

Sonny Insomniac, yeah?

Christine The more you try to sleep, the more awake you feel.

Sonny What do you do? When you can't sleep?

Christine I potter around. I do this and that.

Sonny What?

Christine I chuck bleach down the toilet, I wash the kitchen floor. I get down on my hands and knees and give it a really good scrub. I iron creases out of things.

Sonny You slept on that bed in there.

Christine What do you care, anyway?

Sonny I care.

Christine I thought you weren't coming back.

Sonny You thought I'd done a runner.

Christine It happens.

Sonny I'm here now. Don't you trust anybody?

Christine You've been gone for hours.

Sonny It wasn't hours.

Christine How long's it take to buy a packet of fags round here?

Sonny It wasn't just fags, though, was it? You sent me on a mission.

Christine I was being silly.

Sonny But I made a promise to you, didn't I, to fulfil your every desire.

Christine I was just playing with you.

Sonny Like they say, be careful what you wish for. (*taking a bag of sweets from inside his jacket*) Abracadabra, alacazam. (*He offers her the bag of sweets. She doesn't take them.*) Green. They're all green.

Christine Stop playing with me.

She slaps the packet of sweets out of his hands. They fall on the floor.

Sonny I'm sorry, Christine. I didn't mean to upset you.

Christine You left me on my own.

Sonny I needed some fresh air and the time just went.

Christine You wanted to get away from me.

Sonny If that was true, why did I come back? Eh?

Christine I don't know. I don't know, Sonny. I don't understand what you want from me.

Sonny I want to make you happy.

Christine Why would a beautiful young man like you give a toss about someone like me?

Sonny You're beautiful.

Christine I'm getting old.

Sonny You're at your peak.

Christine Old and ugly. I used to turn heads.

Sonny Beautiful.

Christine You hated kissing me.

Sonny Oh God.

Christine Oh, no offence taken. What did I expect?

Sonny Don't put yourself down.

Christine You could hardly bear to touch me in there. Don't think I didn't notice. You're playing some kind of game with me, aren't you?

Sonny Stop this. It's ugly.

Christine We might as well be honest with each other. What happened in there was a joke. You didn't want me. I seduced you.

Sonny That's not true.

Christine I was the same. I hated old men touching me. And they always found a way. A pat on the knee, a secret stroke of your hand. Their wives beside them, their eyes half-closed like watchful lizards, pretending they weren't aware of what was going on under the table. And you'd be nervous of them, expecting them to shoot out a big rubber tongue to lasso you with across the table. I'd imagine them sitting there chewing me like a fly.

Sonny I did want you.

Christine You say you'll give me anything I want?

Sonny That's what I said.

Christine I want to go to Timbuktu. I want a new identity.

Sonny You gotta run the launderette.

Christine Fuck the launderette. I'd like a new face.

Sonny Yeah? Who'd you want to look like?

Christine Anybody. Why not? Make me look like anybody. How come it's the criminals who get all the money spent on them?

Sonny I'm not a criminal. I've confessed. I been absolved.

Christine And what about the rest of us?

Sonny You don't need absolving. You're innocent, aren't you?

Christine Everybody's got a history.

Sonny Yeah? And what's yours? Eh, Christine? What's your secret?

Christine I haven't got any secrets.

Sonny Tell me why you're so sad.

Christine Sad? Me?

Sonny I want to make you happy.

Christine It doesn't make sense. Life isn't supposed to be like this. Strange men don't just turn up in your launderette just like that, out of the blue, and go out of their way to make you happy.

Sonny Why not? Why not, Christine? Why shouldn't I want to make you happy?

Christine Why me? You could have any girl you wanted. Why did you choose me?

Sonny Because you really are on the run, ent you, just like me.

Christine Is this another game, is it?

Sonny I'll tell you the truth. I've messed my life up, big time. You know the ways a man can mess up, don't you? Something happens and suddenly you're on the wrong track and there's no going back. You understand that, don't you?

Christine I think so.

Sonny You understand. A life can go wrong, Christine. You take a wrong turn and you're lost for ever. You feel like you're running all the time. You daren't look over your shoulder just in case what you're running away from is catching up right behind you. Come on, you know what I'm talking about.

Christine I'm not sure.

Sonny Come on, you know. Stop pretending. I know you. This is the night, Christine, the night when both of us stop running. What have we got to lose? You can tell me anything, anything you want, because you'll never see me again and it might just make you feel better.

Christine It's late and I'm tired. I'm not running away from anything.

Sonny You're running from me right now, hiding, but I can see you. I know who you are.

Christine Yeah? Who am I?

Sonny You're the woman who was in the papers. The woman with the kid.

Pause. Christine is obviously stunned.

Christine What woman? What kid? You've got the wrong person.

Sonny People come in your shop and leave with their hearts lifted, but not you, your heart is never lifted. You remain sad, despite all the joking about and the smiling your eyes never smile. I seen you in the papers – the futile bedside vigil, you saying how you blamed yourself. And I think to myself. If I could do one thing in my life, just one thing that would make me feel good about myself. It would be to make you smile, to make you really smile. With your eyes.

Pause. Christine moves away from him.

Christine You say you wanted to feel good about yourself?

Sonny I wanted to make you happy.

Christine To make yourself feel good.

Sonny That's not what I meant.

Christine It's what you said. You just said that. (*Slight pause.*) You felt sorry for me?

Sonny No, not sorry.

Christine You think my life is shit and you pity me.

Sonny You've got it all wrong.

Christine Oh, I know what you meant. And there's me thinking . . . (*She laughs.*) I'm sorry, Sonny. I've been taking this all far too seriously. (*She laughs.*) Even though you kept telling me it was a joke and I been laughing all day, I still thought . . . I don't want your pity, Sonny. I don't want anybody's pity.

    Christine stands.

Sonny Where you going? Where you going, Christine?

Christine Let me have some dignity, Sonny, yeah? Let me be the one to leave.

    Christine goes into the bedroom. Sonny sits with his head in his hands. Christine comes out of the bedroom, fully dressed.

You'd better have this back.

    Christine gives Sonny back the money he gave her earlier.

Sonny Don't go. Stay one more hour.

Christine A deal's a deal: no strings, you said. (*She makes a move to leave.*)

Sonny I'm like you. I don't like being alone at night. Things start to crowd in on me.

    Pause.

Christine Oh, I think you'll be all right. You've got Mr Walker to look after you. (*She leaves.*)

SCENE THREE

Sonny's flat. It is empty. Everything has been cleared away. Cyrus stands in the middle of the room with Zoe.

Cyrus What's happened?

Zoe They've done a good job, haven't they?

Cyrus Where's it all gone?

Zoe All that needs doing now is to touch up the paintwork. It's uncanny, isn't it? Not a speck of dust anywhere. I wish I could afford for them to do my place.

Cyrus I take it that this is your polite way of telling me to sod off.

Zoe I wouldn't put it quite like that.

Cyrus You never wanted me here in the first place.

Zoe The flat no longer belongs to us. It's council property. You staying here was illegal.

Cyrus I'll just take them bags, then, and I'll be off.

Zoe What bags?

Cyrus Bags, you know, the black bags you put his stuff in.

Zoe There aren't any bags. No stuff, as you put it.

Cyrus What about all his belongings? His things, you know.

Zoe The company I got in were very professional. I told them to be ruthless.

Cyrus You're having fun with me. Ha ha, very funny. Now, please can I have them bags?

Zoe There was no stuff. It was all rubbish.

Cyrus Rubbish? There was records in here, books, papers he'd written notes on. It all meant something.

Zoe Like a code, you mean?

Cyrus If you like, yes.

Zoe I gave you two weeks to crack the so-called code and you didn't do it.

Cyrus Please don't patronise me.

Zoe Look, your . . . investigations – is that what you'd call them? – your investigations have reached a dead end. I've humoured you for days and now enough is enough.

Cyrus Fuck off.

Zoe I'll have those keys back, if you don't mind.

Cyrus You tricked me, took me out for a cup of tea so that they could come in here. You said you had something to tell me.

Zoe It wasn't that calculated. I wanted to talk to you. I tried to tell you, but you kept going on about the woman from the launderette and Sonny's jacket and God knows what else.

Cyrus We had a chance to sort this, to settle it once and for all, and now you've taken all my things away.

Zoe They weren't your things.

Cyrus I had a sleeping bag.

Zoe It was filthy. You'll have to find somewhere else to stay.

Cyrus Behind my back.

Zoe You'd never have let them in, would you? The place stank to high heaven. The council were threatening to come in and do something about it. It's the least I could have done for my brother.

Cyrus What have you done with it all? At least let me have a look at it.

Zoe And what the hell would you do with it?

Cyrus Sort through it. I need to go through it with a fine-tooth comb, I need to find . . . I need to look for . . .

Zoe What? Clues? There aren't any clues. My brother was ill. He must have been. Only a very ill person could have done what he did.

Cyrus He wasn't ill. He was . . .

Zoe Being pursued by a bunch of villains? Come on, surely you don't believe that?

Cyrus I got proof.

Zoe Really? Where from?

Cyrus The woman from the launderette, she told me everything that happened that day, everything he said to her. She said he was happy, telling jokes and playing games. Does that sound like a man about to go under?

Zoe What the hell are you talking about?

Cyrus He's left something behind in this room, something to tell us where he is.

Zoe My brother does not speak to you from beyond the grave. There's nothing left to say.

Cyrus I want his things. You give me his things.

Zoe I gave you the benefit of a doubt and all you come back to me with is some crackpot story.

Cyrus Please just give me his things and I'll go away and look through them on my own.

Zoe Sonny is dead.

Cyrus And now we'll never know what happened to him, will we? You've made sure of that.

Zoe Of course we'll never know. We never could. Even if he left a note it wouldn't tell us anything. That's his secret, locked away in his heart and he's entitled to it. The least we can do is respect that. Villains. Sonny was many things, but he was never a criminal.

Cyrus He chose me. He wanted to tell me something, have me find out what happened to him.

Zoe Why?

Cyrus He wanted me to know so that . . . so that . . .

Zoe So that you wouldn't feel the overwhelming guilt you feel? Well, I'm very sorry, Cyrus, but that's something you're going to have to live with. Just like me and just like Nella.

Cyrus You had it in for me from the start.

Zoe It's all in your mind.

Cyrus You just want to wash your hands of him.

Zoe I want you to stay away from Nella. She's beginning to come to terms with Sonny's death. If you care about her you won't stir things up by telling her all this nonsense.

Cyrus It's my duty to find out what happened to him and I'm going to do that whether you like it or not.

Zoe Stay away from her.

Cyrus I do odd jobs for her.

Zoe And I'm grateful to you. Not least because you've made me aware of how much Robert and me have neglected her, but I plan to put that right now. So, thank you for everything, but now we can manage on our own.

Cyrus She wants me to finish her garden.

Zoe I'll watch Robert closely and make sure he does a good job. I don't want you to even say goodbye to her, do you understand?

Cyrus She'll think I abandoned her.

Zoe She's tougher than she looks. You must have come from somewhere. Maybe it's time you went back there. She'll just assume that you left as suddenly as you arrived.

Cyrus At least tell her that I was called away on urgent business. I don't want her to think that I never cared.

Zoe If that's what you want. Now, give me back the keys.

Cyrus searches in his pocket and produces the keys. He hands them back to Zoe.

You know, Cyrus, you've really helped me. You've helped me to understand that death has no romance to it at all, that it really is just an ending. Nothing more. So, that being the case, the rest of us might just as well get on with the mundane business of living.

SCENE FOUR

Nella's house. The living room. Nella is showing Zoe into the room. As usual Zoe is laden with shopping bags.

Nella You should have told me you were coming.

Zoe I didn't know I was coming.

Nella I'd have got something in.

Zoe There's no need. Look at all this.

74

Nella You shouldn't fuss so much. You need to start caring for yourself.

Zoe It's just a few things, Nella. Why do you have to be like this? Why can't you just let someone do something for you for a change?

Nella That's what I'm saying about you. Why can't I do something for you?

Zoe Like what?

Nella Perhaps I could shop for you and Robert and the kids. It would give me something to do.

Zoe I suppose I just don't like people doing things for me.

Nella See what I mean?

Zoe Perhaps it's the schoolteacher in me. I'm used to being in control.

Nella I know what you mean.

Zoe How did you do it, Nell? How did you manage to spend your days working with demanding brats all day long to come home to demanding brats all evening?

Nella Are you talking about Robert or the kids?

Zoe Both.

Nella You weren't demanding brats.

Zoe I suppose we were all just so grateful to have a home.

Nella All the children I fostered were very polite. It made me feel very guilty. I thought you were afraid of us.

Zoe We were. Well, of *him*, in any case.

Nella He wasn't that bad.

Zoe No, you're right. He was worse.

Nella He'd had a difficult life.

Zoe Hadn't we all?

Nella He loved you all.

Zoe He thought we were a nuisance. He treated us as though he was indulging your little whim.

Nella You talk as though he mistreated you. He never laid a finger on you.

Zoe Exactly. He'd never even look at us.

Nella He was a quiet man.

Zoe He knew how to use silence all right. It was brutal. I loved it when he went out. I used to pray that he'd never come back. And one day he didn't and that was the happiest day of my life.

Nella (*reprimanding*) I loved him, Zoe.

Zoe I know. I'm sorry.

Nella What's got into you?

Zoe Nothing.

Nella It's not like you to talk like this.

Zoe So, what am I like?

Cyrus enters from the garden. He carries a spade and is sweating.

Nella Come in, come in, Cyrus. I'll get you that soup.

Cyrus Soup is just what I need. It's freezing out there.

Nella Don't say I didn't warn you. (*to Zoe*) He's gone mad with digging.

Zoe Digging?

76

Nella I was surprised as well. I thought he'd done a perfectly good job the first time, but he insists that his work wasn't up to scratch.

Zoe goes to the window.

Zoe But it's a mess. You've dug up those beautiful flowers.

Cyrus I'll put it right again.

Nella Look at you, you're shivering. Sit down and I'll get that soup.

Nella goes off.

Zoe What the hell are you doing here, Cyrus? I thought I told you to leave her alone.

Cyrus He was here. He was here in the early hours of that morning. He's buried something in that garden.

Zoe He planted flowers for Nella.

Cyrus He's left something there for me. Everything he did that night, every single thing, he wants me to question, ask questions about and find the answers.

Zoe Why can't you just leave us alone?

Cyrus I'm not going anywhere until this is over and done with.

Zoe It is over and done with.

Cyrus That's what you'd like to think, isn't it? You want his memory out of the way because you think he was Nella's favourite. You're still jealous of him.

Nella returns with a bowl of soup, some bread.

Nella Jealous of who?

Zoe Cyrus thinks that Sonny must have been your favourite.

Cyrus That's not what I said.

Nella Why would he think that? (*to Cyrus*) I had no favourites. I loved them both the same. They were special. (*to Zoe*) The minute I set eyes on you. You were both like sunflowers. You in your little yellow skirt twirling and twirling around for me to see. All those children I fostered and you were the only two I ever adopted. (*to Cyrus*) Why would you want her to think that I favoured Sonny?

Zoe Because he wants to make trouble between us. Tell him to go away. Tell him to stay away from us.

Nella Why should I do that? Cyrus is my friend.

Zoe You have friends. Why do you have this constant need for people like him? Look at the mess he's made out there.

Nella He'll put it right again, won't you, Cyrus?

Zoe You don't know anything about him. He could be a murderer for all you know.

Cyrus Watch what you're saying, Zoe.

Nella Cyrus wouldn't hurt a fly.

Zoe That's what you think.

Nella What are you talking about? Have you two been arguing? What's going on with you two, eh, Sonny? (*realising her mistake*) Did I just say . . . I'm sorry. Cyrus. I meant to say Cyrus.

Zoe And now we have it. Cyrus is right – Sonny was your favourite. Losing Sonny has left a hole in you and you'll look for anything to fill it with. A complete stranger, anything. As long as it's not me.

Nella Nobody could take his place.

Zoe That's right, isn't it? Nobody can fill the hole in you that he's left behind. God knows I've tried. I've tried to make you happy. I've tried to be the daughter you wanted me to be – the good girl. I've passed all the exams, got all the qualifications, and it's still not good enough.

Nella Stop this, Zoe.

Zoe Because I can't take his place, can I? You'd rather replace your boy with a stranger, someone you know nothing about.

Nella Of course I know who he is. We've become very close in the past few months, haven't we?

Cyrus Yes, we have.

Nella I've come to rely on him.

Cyrus It works both ways, Nell.

Nella So, Cyrus is like a son to me. So what? In these past few months he has been a great comfort. He's helped me, Zoe. What's wrong with that? In fact, he's been more of a son to me than you've been a daughter, and that's the truth of it. At least he doesn't place me under the relentless pressure to be cheerful when I am not cheerful.

Zoe You've never been able to judge people, never been able to see what's going on under your own nose. You're like a child who'd go off with a stranger at the drop of a hat. And I'm left to lead the search party to find you and bring you back.

Nella Why don't you go home? Go home, Zoe. Me and Cyrus have things to talk about.

Zoe Are you asking me to leave?

Nella Yes.

Zoe I'll leave you to talk, then.

Pause. Zoe picks up her stuff.

Have you ever wondered why someone as bright and talented as Sonny never fulfilled his promise? Have you ever considered that he never even tried because he knew he wasn't able to live up to your expectations?

Nella Are you saying I drove him to it?

Zoe You wanted him to be your golden boy. If only you knew what he got up to behind your back. But then you never see anything you don't want to see, do you? You want Cyrus to be your confidant and that's what he becomes, never mind that he's been lying to you all this time.

Nella What does she mean, lying to me?

Cyrus Let her go, Nell.

Zoe Don't you remember him? Of course you remember.

Nella Remember him from when?

Zoe Stop playing dumb, Nell. He was at the inquest. He's the train driver.

Nella Don't be silly, Zoe. Of course, he isn't the train driver. The one who . . . that's what you mean, isn't it? Why would that man come here, to us?

Zoe I don't understand it either, Nell.

Nella You're just saying this because you think he's going to take your place. There's no need for all this. You're my very own daughter.

Zoe Why don't you ask him?

Nella Cyrus?

Cyrus doesn't reply.

I tried not to ask myself why a young man like you would be so concerned about an old woman like me, a stranger, but you hear that there are such people in the world, don't you? So, why shouldn't I meet one?

Cyrus I came to take care of you.

Nella You killed my son. Give me back my son. I want my son.

Zoe moves over to comfort her mother.

Don't touch me. Why didn't you tell me?

Zoe You seemed so dependent on him. I was afraid to take that away from you.

Cyrus I just wanted to help you.

Nella Get out of my house. GET OUT OF MY HOUSE.

Cyrus I wanted . . . Sonny wanted me to . . . I wanted to find out about Sonny . . . there were messages, he left messages for me, a trail to find and a father has a duty to a son.

Nella A father?

Cyrus I understand what you feel, Nella, losing a child.

Nella You believe he was your son?

Cyrus We gave him up for adoption. I knew he'd find me one day.

Nella Sonny was not your child. He was mine. Why do you want to take my son away from me?

Cyrus But he's not yours, is he?

Nella Blood means absolutely nothing. You can't just come along, after all these years, and think you can lay claim . . . Besides, I know who his father was.

Pause.

He came here once. Years ago. You remember, Zoe. His father came round on his birthday with a bicycle.

Zoe I can't remember.

Nella He was a Nigerian, I think. He wore a mohair suit and carried a briefcase. You wouldn't go out to meet him. You stayed upstairs in your bedroom, sulking. You said how come Sonny's father comes to visit and mine doesn't.

Zoe I can't remember, Nella.

Nella Sonny wouldn't look at him, remember? He kept patting Sonny on the head and smiling nervously. You could tell he was uncomfortable, couldn't wait to get away. And when he'd gone Sonny took the bike and rode it up and down the garden furiously. He crashed into that tree, remember? He cut his lip.

Pause. Cyrus, devastated, starts to weep silently.

Why didn't you tell him he wasn't Sonny's father?

Zoe I didn't know. He could have been, couldn't he? Maybe I wanted him to be. For Sonny's sake.

Pause. Cyrus picks up his things. He leaves.

Shall I go after him?

Nella Leave him alone.

Zoe We can't let him go out in that state.

Nella He'll be all right. In the long run it's kinder. Come, help me fix this garden.

Zoe It's ruined.

Nella No, it isn't. (*She hands Zoe the spade.*) If we put our backs into it we'll return it to the way it was in no time.

Zoe He'd have hated the garden looking like this. He had an eye for the way things looked, didn't he? (*Slight pause.*) I don't remember Sonny's father, Nell. I don't remember that day with the bicycle. I thought you gave Sonny that bike.

Nella That's the funny thing about memory, isn't it, you can never pin it down. Best leave well alone. Come on, let's get digging.

SCENE FIVE

Nella's garden. Night-time. Nella is standing in the doorway watching as a figure digs the garden.

Nella Surely you can't see what you're doing out there. Come in. It's too late to do the garden. Please come in.

The figure moves into the light and we see that it is Sonny.

Sonny A promise is a promise.

Nella But that was years ago. I wasn't holding you to it.

Sonny Well you should. You should expect far more of people, Nell.

Nella What will the neighbours think? How can you see anything out there?

Sonny I know this garden like the back of my hand, the back of my hand.

Nella Be careful.

Sonny Don't you trust me?

Nella Of course I trust you. (*amused, affectionate*) Isn't this just like you? I don't see you for months on end and then all of a sudden you're in my face gardening at midnight.

Sonny We mustn't let the grass grow under our feet, must we, Nell? We got to seize the moment, live for the day an' all that.

Nella Oh, Sonny, it's so good to see that you're back to your old self again.

Sonny And we'll plant flowers – lots and lots of flowers, what do you fancy?

Nella I have flowers.

Sonny Not these things in pots. Wild flowers, I'm talking about.

Nella When did you last see this garden? There are flowers.

Sonny Don't you wish flowers bloomed overnight like in fairy tales? What was that fairy tale you used to tell me and Zoe?

Nella It wasn't a real fairy tale. I made it up. The one about the brother and sister and the sunflowers.

Sonny You made it up, Nella? You're very talented.

Nella Zoe was here earlier. If only she'd stayed. It would be just like old times. Remember how we'd sit out here on summer evenings? You and your wild ideas and Zoe pooh-poohing them.

Sonny How is Zoe?

Nella Feisty as ever. Fighting hard not to show how vulnerable she is. I wish you two would make up. I'll bet you've both forgotten why you fell out in the first place.

Sonny (*stops cutting*) I haven't forgotten.

Nella I was always falling out with my sister. You'll regret it when you're my age. You can't replace a sister.

Sonny She's not my real sister.

Nella You mean, in the same way that I'm not your real mother? And you're not my real son? You have no idea how much pain it gives me to see you both hating each other.

Sonny We don't hate each other.

Nella You used to be so close. You were inseparable.

Sonny Life moves on. Me and Zoe followed different paths, that's all.

Nella Yes.

Sonny resumes his furious cutting of the garden.

(*laughing*) Take it easy. You'll do yourself an injury. I don't know where you get your energy from.

Sonny It's got to be finished in time.

Nella In time for what?

Sonny I want you to have a beautiful garden to sit out in.

Nella Oh, it's wonderful to see you in such good spirits. You have to admit the last time I saw you you didn't You seem full of life. It makes me very happy.

Sonny I want you to be happy, Nell. I want to make up for all the anxiety I've caused you (*He searches his pockets and takes out some crumpled notes, which he gives to her.*) Here.

Nella What's this?

Sonny You know what it is.

Nella I don't want it.

Sonny Buy yourself something nice.

Nella Isn't it just like you to suggest I buy myself something with my own money?

85

Sonny Here we go.

Nella I don't mean to insult you, but . . .

Sonny I can't do anything right, can I?

Nella It wasn't a loan. I'd rather you had it while I'm still alive to watch you enjoy it. What did you do with the rest of it?

Sonny That's my business.

Nella Of course it is. If you want more you'll have to wait until the morning.

Sonny I don't want more. I don't need money.

Nella You were always very careful. You were scrupulous with pocket money. Zoe would have spent hers within seconds of pay day – do you remember pay days? – but you'd always have some left over till the next week. I was amazed by that. Do you remember that bank you used to run? Zoe still owes you interest on that loan. I remember you declared her bankrupt. I certainly thought you had a future in finance.

Sonny Me in the city? You must be joking. (*He continues digging.*)

Nella Why not? You've got a good brain.

Sonny Let's just forget about it.

Nella Why? You could do so much with your life.

Sonny I said forget it, Nell. And make sure you tell Zoe that debt's been cancelled.

Nella I'm just so pleased to see you.

Sonny There. That's done. What do you think?

Nella Thank you, Sonny.

Sonny Is it all right?

Nella It's wonderful.

Sonny Something nice for you.

Nella I'm happy. Are you happy, Sonny?

Sonny I want to make it up to you.

Nella It's lovely. You've done a really good job. I'm happy.

Sonny You can sit out here and relax, watch the sun go up and down, have a drink. What is it you like to drink?

Nella Chilled white wine. How could you forget that?

Sonny So, I'm forgiven.

Nella Forgiven for what?

Sonny Tell me you forgive me.

Nella But what have you done wrong? Don't tell me you're still churning all this over in your mind. Forget it, Sonny.

Sonny I've tried.

Nella You were always the same, always taking the blame for things you hadn't done, for crimes that hadn't even been committed. I tried to love this guilt out of you but I didn't succeed, did I? It's me who needs to be forgiven. You're so gifted: look at this beautiful garden.

Sonny Something hit the car that night. Something smashed against the car. I felt it.

Nella It could have been anything – a fox or anything.

Sonny I know what's true. And so do you.

Nella You said yourself that you were drunk. I'm not condoning your behaviour but you'll never know what happened. So, why not just forget about it?

Sonny It was raining.

Nella You were soaked through to the skin by the time you came here. Sonny, you must stop tormenting yourself.

Sonny I know what happened. Something died that night.

Nella You must stop this, you must stop this now.

Sonny Something died, and it was my fault.

Nella It was not your fault.

Sonny You're right. It wasn't my fault. It was him. If I hadn't gone to see him it would never have happened.

Nella Sonny, nothing happened.

Sonny You were the one who told me to find him.

Nella So, now it's my turn to get the blame. Yes, I told you to find him. I thought it might set something free within you.

Sonny And I did. I found him.

Nella Yes, you told me.

Sonny I had so much to say to him. I was going to tell him what for, tell him how much I loathed him for ruining my life.

Nella We gave you a good life, didn't we?

Sonny I went to where he works. They showed me where I'd find him. In the canteen, they said. That's him, they said. The one with the loud laugh, and there he was laughing and joking. He had this laugh, Nell, this really loud laugh. And when he laughed he shook his shoulders (*He demonstrates.*) He looked like the kind of bloke everybody liked. And you know something, it wasn't hate I felt. It was more like a longing. Me, a grown man, and all I wanted was for him to hold me. I wanted to say here I am, I'm your son, but I had this feeling that if I did that, he'd just look through me like I was a piece of shit on his shoe. I ran, Nella. I ran away. I wanted to get out. I couldn't get far enough out. In my car in the rain. Running. I couldn't see. Didn't want to see. Something hit my car.

Nella You can learn to forget.

Sonny And then that poor woman in the paper appealing for people to come forward, saying how she blamed herself.

Nella Isn't it just like you to answer someone's plea for help? It wasn't you, Sonny. It was another day, another time.

Sonny Something died.

Nella A fox. There's plenty of foxes in London now, running out into the road. Forget, Sonny, you must forget. It makes me so happy to see you here tonight.

Sonny You have to say that. You have to say that because . . .

Nella Because what, Sonny?

Sonny You're my mother.

Nella is pleased.

Nella I love you, Sonny. You must forget these things. It's time you allowed yourself to forget.

Sonny How can I forget what I can't remember? You don't know me from before, do you? I come to you with no history.

Nella That makes you a lucky man. A man with a clean slate.

Sonny I was with this girl, Nell, and I tried to give her a piece of myself, to make her happy, but I couldn't because there was nothing there. There's something missing.

Nella You only feel this way because you care too much.

Sonny I thought he could tell me what it was.

Nella You should stop caring. Nobody else does.

Sonny I'm sorry, Nella. Take no notice of me.

Nella You're all right, Sonny.

Sonny You're right. I shouldn't care so much.

Nella I'm thrilled to see you.

Sonny I shouldn't have come here. It's too late.

Nella I don't care what time you call round. I'll always want to see you. Why don't you stay over? I'll get you some bedding.

Sonny No. I don't want to put you out. I'm going home.

Nella But it's late.

Sonny I'm going home.

Nella So soon?

Sonny Bye, Mum.

Sonny starts to go, then turns.

You did, you know. You did give me a good life.

He goes.

Nella Sonny.

The dry-cleaner's. Late afternoon. Christine stands behind the counter, which has an artificial Christmas tree on it. There are folded clothes on the counter. Cyrus stands in front of the counter.

Christine I couldn't go home. I walked around the park for a bit and then I had this feeling that I was being followed. Of course there was no one behind me, but by that time I'd got paranoid. The question that kept going through my mind was, how come when someone's nice to me I have to run away from him? What's that all about? Sometimes I go to the airport and watch people coming home. Have you ever done that? The look on people's faces when they first see someone they haven't seen for a long time. Just that total joy. And then you start wondering . . . if they haven't seen each other for so long how're they gonna get on with each other? Does the bickering start on the way home? Or am I just being cynical? Does that light on their faces stay there? Are they really connected? Or does it just seem that way? I've never connected with anybody before. Not before him. A stranger who come in my launderette. (*Slight pause.*) I went back to the hotel room, but he wasn't there. He'd checked out. For a few days after I thought he might come back. I thought he might come back to collect his jacket.

Cyrus He did.

Christine Yes, he did. When I called round the flat the other day and you wasn't there, it was like history repeating itself.

Cyrus I give the keys back to the council. Might as well. I reckon there's some family been on the waiting list for years who'd be glad of that flat.

Christine I hope you didn't leave them all that mess to clear away.

Cyrus Of course not. I cleared it all up.

Christine Thank God for that. I had a job to stop myself from reaching. What time's your train leaving?

Cyrus I don't know.

Christine You don't know? How come you don't know?

Cyrus I don't care.

Christine I'm a state, me. I've got this thing about time. About being on time. When I've got a train to catch or a plane or whatever you won't catch me sitting around.

Cyrus That's because you've always got somewhere to go.

Christine So have you. I thought you was going home.

Cyrus I've been away a long time.

Christine You've got somewhere to go back to.

Cyrus I don't know, Christine.

Christine They say you shouldn't go back. They say you should keep moving forwards, like a train.

Cyrus Who says?

Christine Life's like a train journey. That's what they say, isn't it? (*She laughs.*) Hark at me. (*mocking herself*) Train journey. (*She laughs.*)

Cyrus I got unfinished business.

Christine Haven't we all? The times I've cut and run. It'd take more than a lifetime to tie up all my loose ends. Never look back, that's my motto.

Cyrus I don't know whether I'll be able to fit in again.

Christine So don't go back. Stay here.

Cyrus I've let people down.

Christine That's par for the course. Is it really all over and done with?

Cyrus Yes, it's over.

Christine You solved your puzzle?

Cyrus I haven't got any more questions. Let's put it that way.

Christine What about the gangsters, Mr Walker?

Cyrus Oh, that. That was just a game.

Christine That's what I said. I told you, didn't I?

Cyrus Yes, you told me.

Christine It doesn't feel like it's over to me. It doesn't feel like it'll ever be over.

Cyrus Well, it is. (*attempt at a joke*) We've come to the end of the line.

Christine When you first come in the shop, for a split second I thought you was Sonny; I thought you'd come back. What time d'you say you have to be at the station?

Cyrus I don't know.

Christine You must know what train you're getting.

Cyrus Any one will do.

Christine You're always leaving.

Cyrus Eh?

Christine Like father, like son. You can't just come and go. You can't just leave me hanging like this. I'm not a nothing. Oh, you don't give a damn about anybody else.

Do what you like and damn the consequences for other people.

Cyrus I'm not leaving you. How can I be? There's nothing between us.

Christine I didn't ask to get caught up in all of this.

Cyrus Yes, you did.

Christine I'm just an innocent bystander.

Cyrus Come off it.

Christine Like those poor people standing on the platform when he decided to go under. I'm one a them.

Cyrus You had a choice. He was the one who didn't.

Christine All those people late for work, what should have been an ordinary day disrupted. And for no good reason, as far as I can see. You tell me why he chose me.

Cyrus He didn't choose you. You chose him.

Christine (*quieter*) What do you mean?

Cyrus He recognised you, something in you that he needed.

Christine What did I have that he wanted?

Cyrus Something about you. The way you are. Underneath it all.

Christine How do you know that? (*He doesn't reply.*) Tell me, how do you know that?

   Pause.

Like father, like son.

Cyrus He's not my son. I told you.

Christine I had a kid die.

94

Pause.

Hit and run.

Cyrus I'm sorry.

Pause.

Christine It doesn't stop, does it?

Cyrus Your kid . . .

Christine You'd better get going, hadn't you? I don't wanna keep you. (*ironic*) You might miss your train.

Cyrus The jacket.

Christine What?

Cyrus I've come for the jacket.

Christine You got a ticket?

Cyrus No, I think I lost it.

Christine I'm sorry, but I can't hand over any item of clothing without a ticket. Mr Chakravarty's rules.

Cyrus You know I haven't got a ticket.

Christine And I haven't got your jacket. I give it to the charity shop. You should have said if you wanted to keep it.

Cyrus I'm sorry. I should have said.

Christine I'm sure it's gone to a good home.

Cyrus nods, starts to leave.

It wasn't about the jacket anyway, was it? You were led here. He led you here to me, so that you could look after me.

Cyrus You can take care of yourself.

Christine He wanted you to take care of me.

Cyrus I'm a married man.

Christine Of course you are.

Cyrus I'd better be off, then.

Christine I can usually spot a married man a mile off. They gravitate towards me like heat-seeking missiles. When I was younger that's how I liked it. They'd come and go. Literally. And when they'd leave I'd have this sense of an enormous freedom. You don't look like a married man.

Cyrus I don't, do I? Not any more.

Cyrus leaves. Christine is lost in thought for a moment. Eventually she shakes herself out of it and resumes folding clothes. Aleysha comes from out the back, carrying a plastic carrier bag. She is dressed up to the nines in a very revealing outfit. She tries to sneak past without Christine noticing.

Christine And where do you think you're going, young lady?

Aleysha It's my lunch break.

Christine How long you been round the back?

Aleysha I just got in.

Christine You just got in and now you're going to lunch. Dressed like that.

Aleysha He's taking me to a very posh restaurant.

Christine And you think that's suitable for a posh restaurant?

Aleysha When I say restaurant . . .

Christine You mean the all-day breakfast place up the road.

Aleysha He only gets half an hour for lunch. I want to make an impression.

Christine I think you'll do a lot more than that.

Aleysha (*pleased*) Do you really think so?

Christine You don't know anything about him.

Aleysha You can learn a lot about someone from a service wash.

Christine Really? And what have you learnt about him?

Aleysha Well . . . he's not married.

Christine That's a good start.

Aleysha And he's not into material things. He's more spiritual, I'd say – no designer labels or anything like that.

Christine You mean he's poor.

Aleysha He's sensitive.

Christine He works on a building site.

Aleysha He writes poetry.

Christine He makes up rap lyrics.

Aleysha You're such a snob.

Christine And what do you think our customer would say if she came in and saw you wearing her dress?

Aleysha She's not due to pick it up till Saturday.

Christine What if you damaged it?

Aleysha That's why I've got you, isn't it? You're a genius at invisible mending. And I won't damage it.

Christine You can't go around dressing yourself up in the customers' clothing.

Aleysha Why not? You do it.

Christine That was an emergency.

Aleysha You call going down the newsagent's an emergency?

Christine I'd ripped my trousers. Take it off, Aleysha.

Aleysha Oh, don't be such a tightfist. I'm only wearing it for half an hour. I won't even need to wash it after.

Christine gives her a look.

But I will. With my own fair hands.

Christine Take it off, Aleysha.

Aleysha You're not content with ruining your own life, are you? You want to ruin mine too. He could have been destined to be my future husband.

Christine If it doesn't work out it won't have been your destiny, will it?

Aleysha It definitely won't work out when I turn up in my daggy jeans and T-shirt.

Christine Beauty is in the eye of the beholder.

Aleysha Tell that to Jennifer Lopez.

Christine What if Mr Chakravarty found out? I'd be out on my heel. And so would you.

Aleysha How's he going to find out? You're such a stick-in-the-mud.

Christine I am conscientious and you, my girl, should watch and learn.

Aleysha I'm going to end up sad and lonely in that room upstairs smoking fags and drinking vodka with two-week-old mascara plastered all over my face. I'm going to stink of piss and spend my days festering in my own filth.

Christine Good grief. Where do you get your imagination from? I'm dying of guilt already. Oh, go on then. But make sure you've got it washed and pressed ready for her to pick up on Saturday morning.

Aleysha Thanks, Mum. You won't regret it. You've made me the happiest girl in Islington. You can be my matron of honour.

Christine Don't call me Mum.

Aleysha Why not?

Christine It makes me feel old.

Aleysha You are my mum and you are old. You have to be old so that I can be young.

Christine Thank you very much.

Aleysha You're the best (*emphatic*) Mum.

Christine You little . . .

Aleysha Shall I bring you back a sandwich, Mum?

Aleysha dances around Christine.

Christine If you're not careful I'll tell him about the thumb-sucking.

Aleysha Mum mum mum mum mum.

Christine He'll give up waiting for you if you don't get a move on.

Aleysha Are you trying to get rid of me?

Christine At least then I could get some work done, couldn't I?

Aleysha I'll get my jacket.

Aleysha goes round the back. Christine continues folding clothes. Aleysha comes out again. She's wearing Sonny's jacket.

Christine What you doing wearing that?

Aleysha You was supposed to give it away to the charity shop, but you never. So, I thought I might as well have it. It's smart, ennit?

Christine Take it off.

Aleysha But it goes with the outfit.

Christine It doesn't suit you. You look awful. Take it off.

Aleysha Why?

Christine I said take it off. TAKE IT OFF.

Aleysha removes the jacket, places it on the counter.

Aleysha It's only a jacket.

Christine Look, here. Have this. (*She takes a fur coat out of cellophane, helps Aleysha into it.*) This is much classier. Much more you. You look like Beyoncé in that.

Aleysha What if Mr Chakravarty finds out?

Christine Who's going to tell him? I want my little girl to look good for her date, don't I? Just make sure you don't get mud all over it or anything.

Aleysha I look like a yeti.

Christine You look gorgeous.

Aleysha You sure I won't scare him off in this?

Christine It'll be a good test of whether he's man enough for you.

Aleysha What you gonna do with that jacket?

Christine Nothing.

Aleysha You just gonna keep it hung up like that for ever?

Christine I'm not gonna do anything with it. Go on, off you go.

   Pause.

Aleysha I really miss Dan-Dan.

Christine Yes, me too.

   Pause.

Aleysha He's never gonna come back for that jacket, you know.

Christine I know that. Don't you think I know that? Lover boy'll be wondering where you are. Text me halfway through to let me know how it's going.

   Aleysha smiles weakly. She kisses her mother's cheek and then leaves. Christine is lost in thought for a moment, then she shakes herself out of it. She picks up the jacket, puts it on a hanger and hangs it up on a rack with other dry-cleaned clothes, then gets on with her cleaning. After a little while she goes back over to the rack and removes the jacket. She buries her face in it, smells it. Then she enfolds herself in it, embracing herself with it.

SCENE SEVEN

A train carriage. Cyrus sits on the train as Ernest cleans it.

Cyrus Where is this train going?

Ernest You gots to check the board to find out where the trains go. I don't take no notice. I only clean them.

Cyrus I fancy a long journey to somewhere I've never been before.

Ernest You buy you ticket?

Cyrus I don't know where it's going.

Ernest You gots to buy a ticket.

Cyrus Where do you think I should go?

Ernest How I should know where you have to go? I only clean the trains.

Cyrus You never travel on them yourself?

Ernest Where would I have to go? Everything I need is here in London. What would I be doing going on the train?

Cyrus Don't you want to see the world?

Ernest I don't like the trains. I get bored on a train. Airplane. Now, that's a different story. Give me a long flight and I can stretch out my foot, a glass a champagne and England disappearing under the clouds.

Cyrus So, you can't recommend anywhere?

Ernest By train? I hear Scotland is a pretty place. You going on holiday?

Cyrus Something like that.

Ernest You lucky. Sound like you can go anywhere you want.

Cyrus Yes.

Ernest Nothing tying you down, holding you back.

Cyrus Free as a bird.

Ernest How come you lucky so? I would like that kind of freedom.

Cyrus Would you?

Ernest Of course I would. Wouldn't everybody? Give me my life over again and I wouldn't tie myself down like this.

Cyrus No? What would you do?

Ernest Too many things.

Cyrus Do you remember me?

Ernest I know you?

Cyrus We met before, yes.

Ernest You Miss Claristine's son?

Cyrus A few months ago, we met. On a train like this. On this platform. I was going to Leeds.

Ernest Leeds? That ringing a bell.

Cyrus (*takes money out of his wallet, gives it to Ernest*) Bet you thought you'd never see that again.

Ernest I remember you. The sleeper.

Cyrus I've been here ever since.

Ernest You did look terrible that day, boy – like you seen a lot of bad things. It was a good decision to stay?

Cyrus A lot of things happened.

Ernest And now you back where you started, running away again, leaving all your troubles behind you?

Cyrus Something like that.

Ernest Maybe I should come with you.

Cyrus You're welcome to.

Ernest Why shouldn't I get some of them years back? I could climb a mountain. These legs are still good. Let them all go to hell with their gimme this and gimme that, taking me for granted.

Cyrus Last time I just asked them for a ticket for the next train leaving.

Ernest You must have been in a hurry.

Cyrus I wanted to get away.

Ernest I would like to run away. Maybe I should come with you, to Scotland.

Cyrus Why don't you? I could do with the company.

Ernest Just like that?

Cyrus You said you wanted the freedom.

Ernest I can't afford the ticket.

Cyrus I'll buy you a ticket.

Ernest You would help me like that?

Cyrus I'll buy you a ticket.

Ernest Scotland. Yes, let me climb a mountain. Imagine, you could just jack everything in and start again. Is that what you doing?

Cyrus Something like that.

Ernest You a lucky man. Scotland, though.

Cyrus That's just the beginning. I might go somewhere else.

Ernest But my wife, what would I tell her? My kids . . . Though, maybe if I did go missing they would appreciate me a little more. I don't know if I could do it. You a brave man.

Cyrus I'm starting again.

Ernest You think it's going to be different? This time round?

Cyrus I think so.

Ernest What if it isn't? What if you end up doing all the same things, all over again? You married?

Cyrus Yes, I'm married.

Ernest Three times I married. Three times. To the same woman.

Cyrus You must have loved her.

Ernest No, I marry three different woman, but them all turn into the same wife. I can't believe it. On the wedding night, I'm telling you, I went to bed with a brand new bride, starting everything all over fresh again and wake up the next morning with the self-same woman I marry in 1968. Now, you tell me how that happen. I look at my wife sometimes when she misbehavin' and I think to myself you stay there I can trade you in for somebody nicer, somebody calmer, but deep down I know that I might as well accept that I doom to marry the same woman till eternity.

Cyrus So, you're not coming?

Ernest What's the point? She will just track me down, wherever I go. A man can't escape from a force like that.

Cyrus Maybe you don't want to escape.

Ernest I think you might be right there. I'm happy where I am.

Cyrus You're a lucky man.

Ernest So, you going to Scotland, or where?

Cyrus No, not Scotland.

Ernest Where then?

Cyrus Home. I'm going home.

Ernest I'm glad for you. You have children?

Cyrus Yes.

Ernest That's the best thing, isn't it? Go home. They must be miss you.

Cyrus Will you come with me?

Ernest Me?

Cyrus Maybe you can explain where I've been, what's happened.

Ernest I can't help you, son. You on your own. I done enough explaining for one lifetime.

Cyrus I'm a dead man.

Ernest (*laughs*) I hear you. She going give you hell, eh? What you done so bad?

Cyrus Come with me. She'll cook you dinner. Yes, come with me.

Ernest I never gets involved with husband-and-wife business, not me. Courage, boy. I bet it won't be as bad as you think.

Cyrus No?

Ernest So, you make up you mind at last.

Cyrus Yes. I want to go home. I want to live.

SCENE EIGHT

Sonny sits huddled outside Seven Sisters Tube station, wearing a hoodie. The hood is up so that Cyrus can't see his face. Early morning. Cyrus enters carrying a newspaper and with his holdall slung over his shoulder. He wears a coat over his uniform. He stops when he sees Sonny, smiles and then pretends to walk past, expecting Sonny to say something. When Sonny says nothing he backtracks and repeats his actions. He backtracks again.

Cyrus So what? You gonna make me walk past again?

Sonny What?

Cyrus Ain't you gonna say it this morning?

Sonny Eh?

Cyrus I walk past here every day for two weeks and you say spare some change, you fucking bastard. Every morning you say it.

Sonny Not me.

Cyrus I'm disappointed.

Sonny And do you give it, the change?

Cyrus It's not you.

Sonny No.

Cyrus I thought you was the other bloke.

Sonny He's not here.

Cyrus Nipped in quick and stolen his pitch have you? I heard it's like getting a stall on a market, ain't it?

Sonny I don' t know. I'm new to this. You're disappointed he's not here.

Cyrus He cheers me up. He has a laugh with me, you know what I mean? What's happened to him?

Sonny I don't know.

Cyrus You wonder, you know, when you see someone every day and then suddenly they're gone.

Sonny I'm sure he'll come back.

Cyrus You see him, tell him I said hello.

Sonny I'll do that. I'm sure he'll appreciate it. Do I look like him or something?

Cyrus Not really.

Sonny But you recognised me?

Cyrus I thought you was him.

Cyrus Must be cold in the winter, sitting outside like this.

Sonny I don't notice.

Cyrus Good thing it's so hot at the moment. Otherwise, you'd catch your death.

Sonny That's funny.

Cyrus What is?

Sonny You said I'd catch my death, like someone would throw it to me or like catching a cold or catching someone out. I suppose you never know when it's coming, do you? Unless you've planned it. And even then there's still the element of surprise. I'm being morbid, en I? Is the other bloke more cheerful?

Cyrus He's a bit of a joker, yes.

Sonny So, I'll try to be more like him then.

Cyrus You might make a bit more money.

Sonny Everybody likes a laugh, don't they?

Cyrus (*holds out his newspaper*) You want this? I'm finished with it.

Sonny Does he usually have it, the other bloke?

Cyrus He does, yes.

Sonny Then I'll take it. I'll tell him you asked after him. You going to work?

Cyrus For my sins.

Sonny What sins?

Cyrus I don't know. It's just an expression, ennit?

Sonny The sins of the fathers. You think it's a punishment, your job?

Cyrus It's not easy getting out of bed of a morning, is it? Especially not if you're going to spend your whole day under the ground. It's worse in the winter, I tell you. You get up, it's dark, spend the day in darkness and go home and it's still pitch-black. Like a bloody worm, ennit? An earthworm, that's me.

Sonny Why don't you do something different?

Cyrus Like what?

Sonny Get the Tube to somewhere else, get off at the end of the line, see what happens.

Cyrus You're a joker. I'd get the sack. Is that what you do?

Sonny Sometimes. Why not?

Cyrus Is that what you're doing today?

Sonny I'm thinking about it.

Cyrus No, man. I'd rather be at home helping my wife get ready for this evening. We're having a barbecue. Yeah, a few friends and neighbours, good food – rice and peas, curry goat, rum punch. Family, that's what it's all about, ennit?

Sonny It sounds nice.

Cyrus I got two little girls.

Sonny Yeah? What're their names?

Cyrus Tammy and Jeneka. Two little angels. Devils when they want to be. Makes it all worthwhile though, don't it? You got kids?

Sonny Me? What, with this lifestyle? Nah.

Cyrus Why don't you come tonight? To the barbecue?

Sonny Me? You don't know me.

Cyrus There's lots of people coming I don't know. I invited everybody – the man from the shop round the corner, the postman. My wife's gonna go ballistic. I'm always doing that, but so what? Way I look at it, it's a party, ennit? Everyone's invited as far as I'm concerned.

Sonny Thank you, that's nice, but I can't. I got a prior engagement.

Cyrus Prior engagement. You talk nice, man. Where you go to school? Listen, you need some change? Here, take it (*Takes coins out of his pocket and gives them to Sonny.*)

Sonny Thanks. That's very kind, but I'm all right.

Cyrus Nonsense. Don't be proud, man. We all need a bit of help sometime in our life, don't we?

Sonny (*pockets the change*) You're a very kind person.

Cyrus It's nothing, man. The way I see it you never know when you might need someone to help you out, do you? That could be me sitting there begging change, couldn't it? You change your mind about this evening, just let me know. You know where to find me. Yeah, it's going to be a nice day, man.

Sonny I'm not a beggar, you know.

Cyrus Eh?

Sonny You just assumed . . . because I was sitting out here. I'm waiting for the Tubes to start running.

Cyrus Yeah? So, why did you take my money then?

Sonny I didn't want to embarrass you.

Cyrus So, you took my money? That's false pretences, fraud that is.

Sonny I'm sorry. I didn't mean to trick you or anything.

Pause. Cyrus's serious face suddenly creases into a smile. He starts to laugh, very loudly, shaking his shoulders.

What you laughing at?

Cyrus It's funny.

Sonny I'm just a joke to you, en I? Stop laughing at me. I said stop laughing.

Sonny lurches forward as though to hit Cyrus. who catches him and holds on to him.

Cyrus Hey, hey, man. Take it easy.

Cyrus keeps hold of Sonny. There is a moment of tenderness between them, a sense of connection, which transcends space and time. Eventually Cyrus lets Sonny go.

I was just having a joke with you. You can give the money back if you want.

Sonny fishes in his pocket and takes out coins, which he gives to Cyrus.

You can keep the paper. Something to read while you're waiting, eh?

Sonny rolls up the newspaper.

It must be rough on the streets. I suppose you've always got to be watching your back just in case, but you should watch that temper, you know. You might lash out at the wrong person. You all right?

Sonny Yeah, yes, I'm all right. I'm sorry.

Cyrus Forget about it. It's you I'm worried about.

Sonny I'm all right.

Cyrus You don't wanna be getting into fights, not round here.

Sonny Really, I'm all right. I didn't mean to . . .

Cyrus No hard feelings, mate. I don't like being laughed at either. Listen, I'm going in the canteen. I never start work without a full English breakfast inside me. Full English breakfast with fried dumplings and plantain on the side. The wife reckons I'll have a heart attack I'm not careful. What's she know? Let me buy you breakfast.

Sonny No, mate, you're all right.

Cyrus There's a special discount for staff.

Sonny I don't want you to buy me anything.

Cyrus All right. I was just offering, that's all.

Pause.

Listen, Jumping Jack Flash or Fish in the Sea? Choose one. Go on.

Sonny Fish in the Sea.

Cyrus Right, that's what I thought. It's got a lucky ring, ennit? That's the one I'm gonna put a bet on at lunch time.

Sonny Good luck.

Cyrus You take care of yourself. And no more fights, yeah? Laters.

Sonny Laters.

Cyrus starts to go. Sonny watches him leaving. Cyrus turns around and catches Sonny staring. Sonny is embarrassed and looks down at the ground. Cyrus stands there watching Sonny.

End.